International Mathematics

Teacher's Guide 1

International **Mathematics**

Teacher's Guide 1

Andrew Sherratt

HODDER
EDUCATION
PART OF HACHETTE LIVRE UK

Hachette Livre UK's policy is to use papers that are natural, renewable and recyclable products and made from wood grown in sustainable forests. The logging and manufacturing processes are expected to conform to the environmental regulations of the country of origin.

Orders: please contact Bookpoint Ltd, 130 Milton Park, Abingdon, Oxon OX14 4SB. Telephone: (44) 01235 827720. Fax: (44) 01235 400454. Lines are open 9.00–5.00, Monday to Saturday, with a 24-hour message answering service. Visit our website at www.hoddereducation.co.uk.

© Andrew Sherratt 2008
First published in 2008 by
Hodder Education, part of Hachette Livre UK,
338 Euston Road
London NW1 3BH

Impression number	5	4	3	2	1
Year	2012	2011	2010	2009	2008

Cover photo © Alan Schein Photography/Corbis
Illustrations for this title were produced by Barking Dog Art
Typeset in 11.5/14.5pt Garamond by Charon Tec Ltd (A Macmillan Company)
Printed by Martins the Printers, Berwick upon Tweed, UK

A catalogue record for this title is available from the British Library

ISBN 978 0 340 96745 4

Contents

Author's foreword

These books started their life during the years I spent teaching maths in Thailand. When I arrived at my first school, I was handed a syllabus (in Thai!) and told to get on with it. This school had no textbook upon which the syllabus was based, and I soon discovered why – all the English-language maths textbooks I found were written for native speakers of the language.

Most people find maths a challenge at the best of times, but trying to study it in a foreign language steps up this challenge enormously. When you add a reference book that uses uncompromising language designed for native speakers, it all becomes pretty impossible!

I started to write material for each unit I was teaching, using the simplest and most straightforward language and explanations I could manage. It was not meant to replace good, clear teaching in class; rather it was reference material that my pupils could use, with the aid of a dictionary, for self-study.

Through contact with other ESL/EFL maths teachers, I know that my experience has not been unique. Throughout the world there are teachers of ESL/EFL maths struggling to find simply-worded, straightforward textbooks for their pupils – I hope this series will meet that need.

Introduction

Maths syllabi for Years 7, 8 and 9 (approximately ages 11 to 14/15) vary from country to country. For this reason, it would be nearly impossible to write books that covered each country's syllabus exactly. However, the basic topics covered during these years in each country are, in most cases, very similar. This series has therefore been designed to cover the most common topics taught to pupils in this age group around the world.

The spread of topics over the three Coursebooks in this series is designed to build pupils' knowledge in graduated stages. For example, it would be very difficult to discuss addition of fractions without already having covered the idea of multiples, and the least common multiple in particular; so Unit 3 (Fractions) of Coursebook 1 builds on Unit 2 (Factors and multiples). At the same time, there are of course topics that stand fairly independently and you may choose to include these in the work for any year, as best suits the needs of your country or school.

The first book in the series is designed to build a firm and solid foundation for pupils in all the basic techniques used in the main branches of mathematics (except trigonometry, which is introduced in the third book).

Some of the work covered in this first book (especially in the earlier units) involves topics that pupils should have mastered long before they reach this level in their education. This may, however, be the first time they have been exposed to the topic in English.

It is easy to focus entirely on the teaching of the maths and lose sight of the essential process of ESL/EFL teaching, which should take place alongside the maths. To a certain extent, maths is the easiest subject to teach in the ESL/EFL context, since much of the 'language' of maths is common throughout the world; in my opinion, however, the belief that it is possible to learn the intricacies of maths without much need for any specific language of communication is incorrect. An ESL/EFL maths teacher who does not carefully manage the dual strands of both maths teaching and English language teaching risks jeopardising their pupils' progress in mastering new concepts in maths – the pupils may have to try so hard to unravel the English used that they cannot assimilate the maths as well.

Education styles

With their simple approach and no-nonsense style, these books are intended as an honest and reliable source of maths teaching and learning material. The teaching notes include lists of the main skills that pupils should have mastered by the end of each unit, but the books do not commit teachers to particular lesson plans; rather they provide reference material and practice exercises that pupils from any language and cultural background are able to understand easily. You should embellish this core material with whatever colour, flare and entertainment that might be appropriate to the country and culture in which you are teaching.

Teaching hours

Since the total number of teaching hours available in a year for maths will vary greatly from country to country, and school to school, it is difficult to specify how much time should be devoted to any given topic. For this reason, a percentage of the total teaching hours available has been allocated to each unit.

Equipment

For most units you will need only a chalkboard or whiteboard to write on; any other requirements are listed in the notes for the unit.

Teaching vocabulary

Some teachers in the ESL/EFL world find it useful to pre-teach any new vocabulary before teaching the new topic. Others prefer to introduce the new concept first, using vocabulary the pupils are already familiar with, and then adding the names for these new concepts. This is entirely a personal choice and there are valid arguments for both approaches to the teaching of ESL/EFL maths.

My preference is for the second approach: I believe that mastery of the English language is an essential skill for an ESL/EFL maths teacher, so that they are able to explain any concept in many different ways, using only the simplest of vocabulary, and sentence constructions with which the pupils are already comfortable. It should not be necessary to use new vocabulary until after you have explained the new concept. In this way, the pupils need focus on only one thing at a time – first understanding the new maths, and then learning the new English vocabulary that will help them to be more specific and concise when talking and reading about this new maths.

Whichever approach you choose, encourage your pupils to produce their own reference book containing all the new vocabulary they learn: turn a regular exercise book into a 'wordbook' by adding an alphabetical index down the side. Each time a new piece of vocabulary is introduced, pupils should add it to their wordbook, together with their own explanations. Wordbooks work best if they do not reproduce a dictionary explanation or translation: encourage pupils to make it very personal, and to use any means they like to help them to remember what the word means and how to use it. These can include:

- a translation into their own native language
- a drawing or a picture
- an example of how it is used.

It is of course important to keep up with the entries of new vocabulary on a regular basis. To help pupils with this, you might like to set aside a strip of a board in their classroom for new vocabulary. You can then write the new words met in each lesson in this space on the board, and pupils can copy them into their wordbooks, adding their own explanations.

The key vocabulary for each unit is given at the beginning of the unit in the Coursebook, and repeated in this Teacher's Guide. Pupils need to understand all the terms in the unit's list in order to master the unit of work in the medium of English.

Pupils' proficiency in the English language varies greatly from class to class. If you are facing pupils who have studied only basic English up to this point, you may find it helpful to spend some time in the first few lessons building their confidence in the new medium of instruction for their maths lessons. One way to do this is to take a look at the essential maths equipment used regularly and learn the vocabulary associated with this equipment (see the worksheets on pages xii–xiii).

The answers

Pupils' answers to exercise questions should, of course, be checked: doing so allows both teacher and pupils to gauge how well the topic has been understood. The answers can be checked in many different ways; each method has its own advantages and disadvantages, and how each teacher chooses to check their pupils' work is a highly personal decision.

When teaching maths in an ESL/EFL environment, however, you may find it particularly helpful to give the answers orally in class. This may seem to use a lot of class time, but it gives the pupils essential and regular practice in listening to and understanding maths in English – remember that any calculations written down will be read and understood by the pupils in their native language by default. Interaction with your pupils during this oral marking of the exercises should alert you to any problems, and you can then explain answers in more detail on the board if necessary. You could also walk around the class and carefully scrutinise the pupils' work while you are reading out the answers: this will enable you to identify individual pupils' difficulties, which can then be addressed either collectively or individually, as appropriate.

Word problems

I believe that word problems are one of the best ways for pupils to develop and apply their knowledge of the maths techniques they have learned. Of course, word problems present greater challenges for ESL/EFL pupils than for those studying maths in their native language: they need to understand the words and the story before they can even begin to decide what maths techniques they will use to work out the answer.

In these books, word problems are presented using very simple language and vocabulary. However, pupils should get into the habit of using a dictionary to make sure they understand the story contained in the problem, before beginning any calculations.

It is important that pupils do not answer word problems using just numbers: they must include the units of the answer to show that they understand what they have worked out. Errors may indicate that they have understood the maths, but not the English. For example, if a pupil is working out the total number of pupils in Year 7, an answer of 147 may be numerically correct, but has the pupil really understood the question? An answer of '147 pupils' suggests that they have; '147 classes' indicates that there is a problem. All too often, pupils get the general 'drift' of a problem and are able to make a pretty good guess at the maths they need to do to come up with the answer. Then, without a proper understanding of the language and story involved, they simply choose a word at random from the problem to attach to the answer, showing that they don't really understand what they have worked out. Insisting that word problems are not answered using just numbers will enable you to help your pupils understand the English as well as the maths.

Icons

Throughout the Coursebook and Workbook, you will see that calculator icons have sometimes been placed next to an exercise. Where there is *no* icon, it can be left to the teacher's discretion whether or not pupils use a calculator to complete the questions. The icons have only been used to indicate exercises where pupils specifically should or should not use a calculator.

Maths equipment

Name: _____

Class: _____

Maths equipment

Name: _____

Class: _____

Draw an arrow (———►) to join the correct boxes.
The first one has been done as an example for you.

We draw straight lines with	an eraser
We measure angles with	a pencil
We draw a circle with	a ruler
We keep sheets of paper in	a protractor
We erase mistakes in pencil with	a pencil sharpener
We draw pictures and diagrams with	a set square
We cut paper with	a pen
We erase mistakes in pen with	a folder
We fix papers together securely with	a pair of scissors
We attach pictures to a notice board with	liquid paper
We work out calculations with	thumbtacks
We sharpen a pencil with	paperclips
We stick pieces of papers together with	a calculator
We write with	a stapler
We can draw triangles with	a piece of tape
We hold papers together for a short time with	a pair of compasses

Unit 1 Integers

Most of your pupils will already know about the basics of addition, subtraction, multiplication and division of whole numbers – in their home language! In my opinion, the challenge of reaching the same level of proficiency in basic arithmetic in the medium of English is often considerably underestimated. The focus of this unit is therefore not on learning new maths techniques, but on creating every possible opportunity for pupils to revise these essential basic techniques while they are learning their English numbers and all the associated vocabulary. You can help pupils with this by

- holding regular pop quizzes in the form of oral mental arithmetic questions. This gives invaluable practice in recognising and understanding the numbers and operations in English and in carrying out arithmetic mentally. It is the need for a back-and-forth mental translation process that makes English mental arithmetic difficult for pupils: plenty of practice will eventually reduce this need
- setting pupils to work in pairs, asking each other multiplication and division questions based on the multiplication table. This gives them practice in both speaking and calculating in English.

Key vocabulary

add	negative sign
addition	number
ascending	number line
bigger	numeral
biggest	odd
billion	operation
borrow	order
bracket	parts
column	place value
counting numbers	positive
descending	positive sign
difference	product
digit	quotient
divide	remainder
division	short division
equal	short multiplication
equation	smaller
even	smallest
figure	subtract
integer	subtraction
less	sum
long division	symbol
long multiplication	tables
million	thousand
minus	unit
more	value
multiplication	whole number
multiply	zero
negative	

Teaching and learning objectives

After studying the work covered in this unit, pupils should be able to

- recognise whole numbers (both positive and negative) and name them in English, recognise even and odd numbers, and show all these numbers on number lines
- recognise and name the place value of any digit in a whole number
- compare the sizes of integers and use the symbols < and > to write integers in ascending and descending order
- perform accurate addition and subtraction of integers (both positive and negative) and show these calculations on number lines
- perform accurate multiplication and division of integers (both positive and negative)
- perform the four basic mathematical operations in the correct order when calculating with integers
- understand simple word problems in English (with the aid of a dictionary) and be able to apply the maths skills they have learned to work out the correct answer to the problem.

Teaching hours

You should aim to devote approximately $12\frac{1}{2}\%$ of your total annual teaching hours to this unit.

The journey through Unit 1

POSITIVE WHOLE NUMBERS + **NEGATIVE WHOLE NUMBERS**

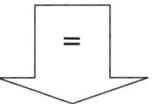

INTEGERS

Numerals, digits and numbers

Counting numbers = positive whole numbers + 0

Place value Digits have different sizes in different places.

Reading and writing numbers in English Name digits in groups of three, starting at the right. Each group of three has a special name.

Odd and even numbers

Writing numbers in order

– ascending
– descending

The number line A great help to pupils when learning addition and subtraction

Addition

Word problems

Subtraction

Multiplication and Division Pupils should learn the multiplicatoin table and practise it often so that they don't need to translate back and forth into their native language.

Properties of positive whole numbers

The order of operations It is very important that everyone follows the same rules, or the answers will be different! Lots of practice is recommended.

When do we use negative numbers?

Writing integers in order

Addition and subtraction of integers Use a number line to practise – it makes it much easier to master this work with negative numbers as well as positive ones.

Multiplication of integers Multiply the signs first. Then multiply the numbers as before.

Division of integers Divide the signs first. Then divide the numbers as before.

Unit 2 Factors and multiples

This section of work is really about how numbers are connected – we can multiply or divide numbers to make other numbers. It is very useful to be able to recognise quickly whether one number is a factor or a multiple of another.

Teaching and learning objectives

After studying the work covered in this unit, pupils should be able to

- find all the factors of a given number
- write any multiple of a given number
- test the divisibility of a number by 2, 3, 4, 5, 9 and 10
- recognise all the prime numbers smaller than 100
- write any number as the product of its prime factors
- determine the HCF of any two or more numbers
- determine the LCM of any two or more numbers
- understand simple word problems in English (with the aid of a dictionary) and be able to apply the maths skills they have learned to work out the correct answer to the problem.

Teaching hours

You should aim to devote approximately $12\frac{1}{2}\%$ of your total annual teaching hours to this unit.

Key vocabulary

common factor	lowest/least common multiple (LCM)
common multiple	multiple
composite number	power
cubed	power number
divisibility	prime factor
divisible	prime factorisation
factor	prime number
highest common factor (HCF)	product
index	squared
index notation	

The journey through Unit 2

Factors

Multiples
'Multiple' comes from 'multiply' – so you get a **bigger** number.

Tests of divisibility
These can save a lot of time.

Prime numbers
These have only **two factors** – the number and 1.

Prime factors
Every number can be written as the product of prime factors.

Index notation
This is only a brief introduction to this way of writing numbers – see Unit 5 for more.

Highest common factor (HCF)

Lowest (least) common multiple (LCM)

Fractions

Units 3 and 4 cover basic but vital techniques that most pupils will have encountered in previous years of school study.

In both units, the emphasis is once again on revising the maths and practising it in the context of the English language. The more competent a pupil is with this sort of foundation work, and the more comfortable they are dealing with it in English, the easier they will find it to study all the subsequent new work. Don't be tempted to rush through these two units simply because your pupils seem to be confident of the maths – make every opportunity for them to become equally confident with it all in English.

A short oral quiz at the beginning of a class will help your pupils to gain confidence in the English names of fractions and how to calculate them quickly. Again, the aim is to reduce the need for translation back and forth into their native language.

Teaching and learning objectives

After studying the work covered in this unit, pupils should be able to

- recognise fractions as numbers in the form of a numerator divided by a denominator
- give any fraction an English name
- recognise and name a proper fraction, an improper fraction and a mixed number
- convert an improper fraction into a mixed number and vice versa
- write any fraction in its equivalent forms
- reduce fractions to their lowest terms

- compare the sizes of fractions and use the symbols $<$ and $>$ to write fractions in ascending and descending order
- perform accurate addition, subtraction, multiplication and division of fractions
- perform the four basic mathematical operations in the correct order when calculating with fractions
- understand simple word problems in English (with the aid of a dictionary) and be able to apply the maths skills they have learned to work out the correct answer to the problem.

Teaching hours

You should aim to devote approximately $12\frac{1}{2}\%$ of your total annual teaching hours to this unit.

Key vocabulary

cancel	invert
decrease	lowest terms
denominator	mixed number
equal	numerator
equivalent fractions	ordinal numbers
first	part
formula	proper fraction
fraction	quarter
half	reduce
improper fraction	second
increase	simplify
inequality	third

The journey through Unit 3

What is a fraction?
Part of a number

Shaded fractions
Showing fractions as shaded parts of a shape

Parts of a fraction ⟹ $\dfrac{\text{numerator}}{\text{denominator}}$

Ordinal numbers ⟹ **Naming fractions in English**
– Use counting numbers for the numerator
– Use ordinal numbers for the denominator
or
Counting number **over** counting number

Types of fractions ⟹
– proper fractions
– improper fractions
– mixed numbers

Mixed numbers ⟺ changing ⟺ **Improper fractions**

Equivalent fractions
They are all the same fraction when written in their **lowest terms**.

Comparing fractions ⟹
– ascending order
– descending order

Addition and subtraction of fractions
Using the LCM of denominators to write equivalent
fractions that can be added and subtracted

Multiplication of fractions

Division of fractions
Changing the ÷ sign into a × sign and writing the
fractions after the ÷ sign upside down

The order of operations with fractions ⟹
– brackets
– multiplication and/or division
– addition and/or subtraction

Solving word problems with fractions

Unit 4 Decimals

As mentioned in the notes for Unit 3, this work on decimals is very important as a foundation for future topics. Don't assume that pupils who find the actual maths quite straightforward are automatically comfortable with the required English.

Take time to create as many opportunities as possible for pupils to practise all aspects of working with decimals in English – regular oral quizzes and paired work are just two of the many ways to do this.

Teaching and learning objectives

After studying the work covered in this unit, pupils should be able to

- recognise and name the place value of any digit in any decimal number
- give any decimal number an English name
- write all decimal numbers in expanded form
- compare the sizes of decimal numbers and use the symbols $<$ and $>$ to write decimals in ascending and descending order
- perform accurate addition, subtraction, multiplication and division of decimals
- perform the four basic mathematical operations in the correct order when calculating with decimals

- convert decimals into fractions and fractions into decimals or recurring decimals
- recognise recurring decimals and write them using the correct notation
- understand simple word problems in English (with the aid of a dictionary) and be able to apply the maths skills they have learned to work out the correct answer to the problem.

Teaching hours

You should aim to devote approximately $12\frac{1}{2}\%$ of your total annual teaching hours to this unit.

Key vocabulary

decimal	divisor
decimal fraction	expanded form
decimal place	pattern
decimal point	place value
decimal whole number	recurring decimal
dividend	repeating decimal

The journey through Unit 4

Place value
Revision

Decimals
When we use the word 'decimal', we often mean 'decimal **fraction**'.

Understanding decimal numbers
The decimal point and decimal places
Showing the place value of each digit by writing the number in expanded form

Comparing decimals 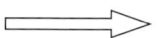 – ascending order
– descending order

Addition and subtraction of decimals
Adding and subtracting digits with the same place values

Multiplying and dividing decimals by power of 10
Moving the digits to the left or the right

Multiplication of decimals
The total number of decimal places before multiplying = the total number of decimal places after multiplying

Division of decimals
Always change the divisor into a whole number by moving the decimal point.
Remember to move the decimal point in the dividend exactly the same number of places.

Decimal (fractions)  changing **Fractions**

Recurring (or repeating) decimals
Some fractions change into recurring decimals.

Unit 5   Power numbers

The purpose of this unit at this point in the book is to provide pupils with the essential basic tools for dealing with power numbers and their multiplication and division. A unit in a subsequent book in this series will deal comprehensively with all the index laws and related work.

Key vocabulary

base	power form
index	power number
index form	scientific notation
index notation	standard form
indices	standard index form
power	

Teaching hours

You should aim to devote approximately $3\frac{1}{2}\%$ of your total annual teaching hours to this unit.

Teaching and learning objectives

After studying the work covered in this unit, pupils should be able to

- write a number in index form using a given base
- perform accurate multiplication and division of numbers with powers
- write any number in standard index form and vice versa
- perform accurate multiplication and division of numbers in standard form
- understand simple word problems in English (with the aid of a dictionary) and be able to apply the maths skills they have learned to work out the correct answer to the problem.

The journey through Unit 5

Index form
A short way to write many of the same number multiplied together
Any number with a zero index is equal to 1

$\longrightarrow$

(base number)^index number

Multiplying and dividing numbers with powers
Multiplying: add the index numbers
Dividing: subtract the index numbers

Standard (index) form
A short way to write very big or very small numbers

Multiplying and dividing numbers in standard form

Unit 6 Other number systems

The system of Roman numerals is used widely in most English-language countries. For this reason, it is useful for pupils to be able to read and write Roman numbers.

The unit also includes a brief overview of some other number systems. Some of them were used historically, while others are still used regularly today, either in addition to the 'international' Arabic numbers or, in some cases, instead of them. You may decide to spend more or less time on these other systems depending on how applicable they are to the country and culture within which you are teaching.

Teaching and learning objectives

After studying the work covered in this unit, pupils should be able to

- appreciate the history of number systems other than the Arabic numbers
- write any modern Arabic number smaller than 4000 in Roman numerals
- write any Roman numeral smaller than 4000 in modern Arabic numbers.

Teaching hours

You should aim to devote approximately $1\frac{1}{2}\%$ of your total annual teaching hours to this unit.

Key vocabulary

Arabic numbers	Roman numerals
Latin digits	symbol
lower case	upper case
mathematical operations	

The journey through Unit 6

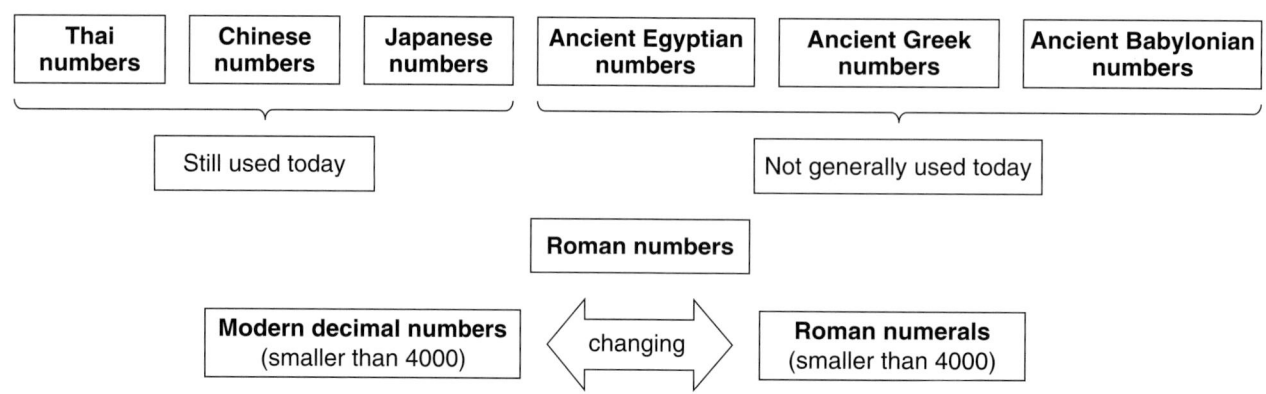

Approximation and estimation

Until now, the focus of all the maths pupils have studied has been on accuracy: some pupils may therefore find the idea that some answers are not fully accurate, or that there may be more than one 'correct' answer (or indeed no correct answer) to a problem, very difficult. The introduction of 'degrees of accuracy' blurs the lines further, so you should expect at least some of your pupils to find this topic quite challenging.

In some countries, maths is traditionally seen as a subject in which there is one correct answer to every question. This clearly makes approximation and estimation more difficult for pupils to understand. It is therefore important to understand the language and cultural context in which you are teaching – despite the 'universal' or 'international' image of mathematics.

Teaching and learning objectives

After studying the work covered in this unit, pupils should be able to

- round any number to the nearest given power of 10
- round any number to a given number of decimal places
- round any number to a given number of significant figures
- round in real-life situations, giving the most 'sensible' answer
- estimate the answer to a calculation
- understand simple word problems in English (with the aid of a dictionary) and be able to round off the answer in the most sensible way appropriate to the real-life situation.

Teaching hours

You should aim to devote approximately $7\frac{1}{2}\%$ of your total annual teaching hours to this unit.

Key vocabulary

accurate	estimation
approximate	exact
approximation	round
degree of accuracy	significant figure
estimate	

The journey through Unit 7

APPROXIMATION

This is done after you finish a calculation.
Use it to write a simpler answer.

Rounding to the nearest power of 10

Rounding using decimal places

Rounding using significant figures
Remember to keep the rounded number the same size
– add zeros if necessary.
Remember which zeros are significant and which are not.

Rounding and real-life problems

ESTIMATION

This is done before you do a calculation.
Use it to work out an answer that is close to the exact one.

Estimating an answer
Round off every number to 1 significant figure.
Perform the calculation with these simpler numbers.

Measures and measurement

The work covered in this unit is intended as an introduction to the concept of measuring some aspects of the 'size' of things. When pupils have mastered the basic tools used in measurement, they will be ready for future units covering the measurement of plane figures and 3-dimensional solid figures.

This unit also forms a very basic foundation for geometry which, of course, literally means 'to measure the world'.

Equipment

As well as a chalkboard or whiteboard to write on, you might find the following equipment useful.

- Large clock-face with moveable hands that you can position to show different times.
- Large-sized ruler that you can use with your chalk/whiteboard.
- Scale to measure the weights of some objects.
- Measuring jug or other containers useful for measuring and showing the volumes of some liquids.

Key vocabulary

a.m.	metre
approximate	Metric system
capacity	midday
centimetre	midnight
century	milligram
day	millilitre
decade	millimetre
decimetre	minute
estimate	month
gram	noon
heavy	o'clock
height	p.m.
hour	second
Imperial system	speed
kilogram	time
kilometre	tonne
leap year	unit
length	volume
litre	week
long	width
mass	year
measure	

Teaching and learning objectives

After studying the work covered in this unit, pupils should be able to

- convert one unit of time into any other unit of time
- convert any time written in the 12-hour clock to a time written the 24-hour clock and vice versa
- calculate the amount of time between two given times on the same or on different days
- convert one metric unit of length to any other metric unit of length
- convert one metric unit of mass to any other metric unit of mass

- convert one metric unit of volume to any other metric unit of volume
- estimate the length, mass or volume of an object using common known objects as measures
- understand simple word problems in English (with the aid of a dictionary) and be able to apply the maths skills they have learned to work out the correct answer to the problem.

Teaching hours

You should aim to devote approximately $7\frac{1}{2}\%$ of your total annual teaching hours to this unit.

The journey through Unit 8

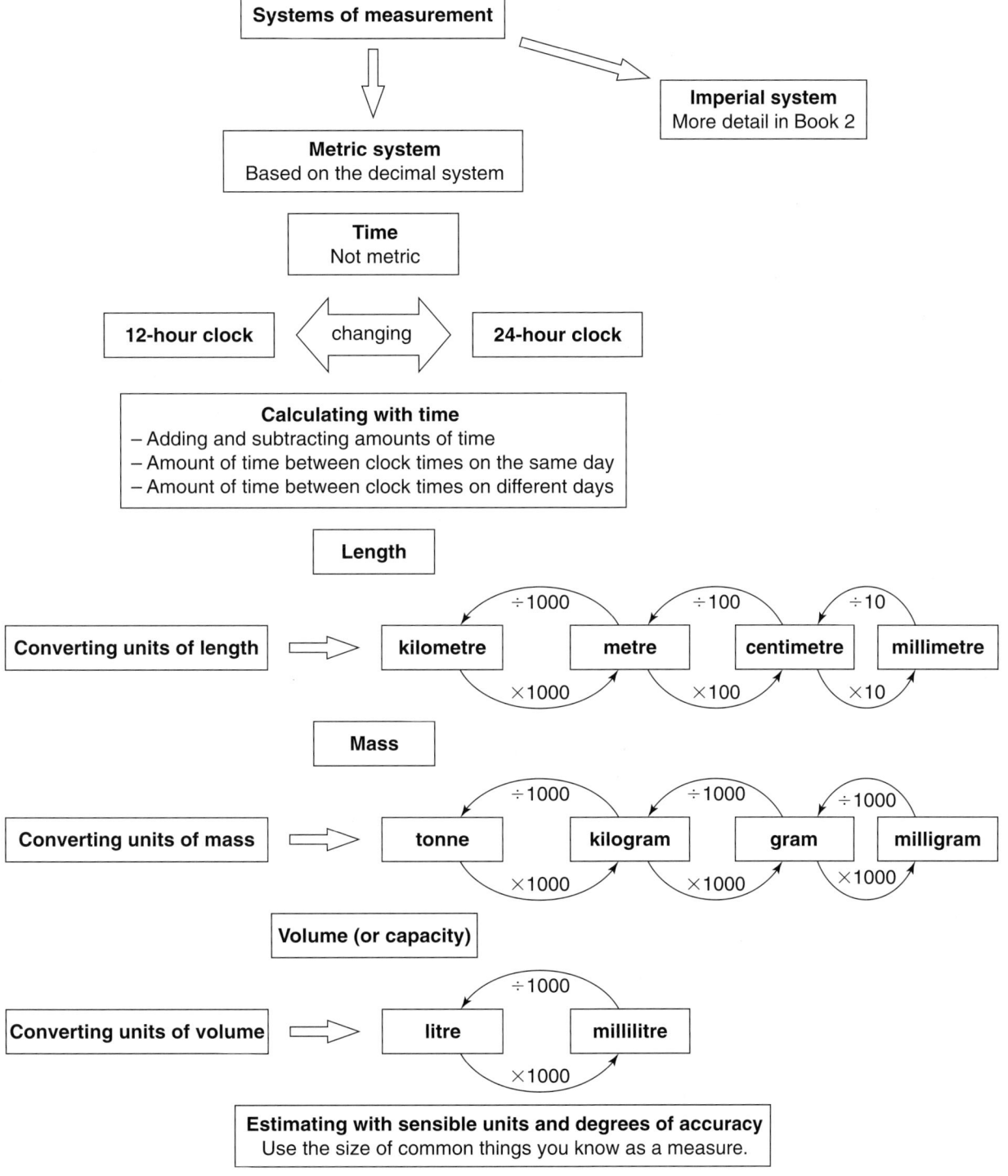

Systems of measurement

Imperial system
More detail in Book 2

Metric system
Based on the decimal system

Time
Not metric

12-hour clock ⟷ changing ⟷ 24-hour clock

Calculating with time
– Adding and subtracting amounts of time
– Amount of time between clock times on the same day
– Amount of time between clock times on different days

Length

Converting units of length ⟹

| ÷1000 | ÷100 | ÷10 |

kilometre — metre — centimetre — millimetre

| ×1000 | ×100 | ×10 |

Mass

Converting units of mass ⟹

| ÷1000 | ÷1000 | ÷1000 |

tonne — kilogram — gram — milligram

| ×1000 | ×1000 | ×1000 |

Volume (or capacity)

Converting units of volume ⟹

| ÷1000 |

litre — millilitre

| ×1000 |

Estimating with sensible units and degrees of accuracy
Use the size of common things you know as a measure.

An introduction to algebra

In my opinion, this is probably the single most important topic you will teach your pupils. Unfortunately, algebra is notorious among pupils – too often they believe it is very difficult even before they begin to study it.

If your pupils are to progress confidently and successfully through the rest of the maths they must learn at school, it is important that they master the skills of algebra. It is your job to find effective ways of overcoming the fears that surround this branch of maths and to enable your pupils to grasp the basic concept that letters of the alphabet can stand in place of unknown numbers in maths calculations – in a nutshell, this is the essence of algebra!

The fundamental building blocks contained in this unit are very important. Don't be tempted to rush through them, or try to introduce more complex algebraic manipulations than those covered in this basic unit of work – pupils will be able to make more rapid and confident progress with more complex algebra only when they truly understand how to use these basics.

I use the analogy of algebra being the 'language of maths' – with 'words' and 'sentences'. I find pupils are able to relate to this and grasp the new vocabulary and how it all fits together more easily. The most important thing is to find

whatever method works for you and your pupils – the more confident you are about algebra and the more simply you can explain things, the more your pupils will find their apprehension turns into comprehension.

Key vocabulary

addition	minus sign
algebra	multiplication
algebraic expression	plus sign
bracket	product
coefficient	quotient
constant	simplify
constant term	substitute
difference	subtraction
distributive law	sum
division	symbol
evaluate	term
expand	unlike terms
expansion	variable
expression	variable term
like terms	

Teaching and learning objectives

After studying the work covered in this unit, pupils should be able to

- translate any maths calculation written in words into an algebraic expression
- evaluate algebraic expressions
- distinguish between terms, variables, coefficients and constants in algebraic expressions
- distinguish between like terms and unlike terms in algebraic expressions
- simplify algebraic expressions by combining like terms
- add and subtract algebraic expressions
- multiply and divide one term by another term
- use the distributive law to expand brackets in algebraic expressions.

Teaching hours

You should aim to devote approximately 15% of your total annual teaching hours to this unit.

The journey through Unit 9

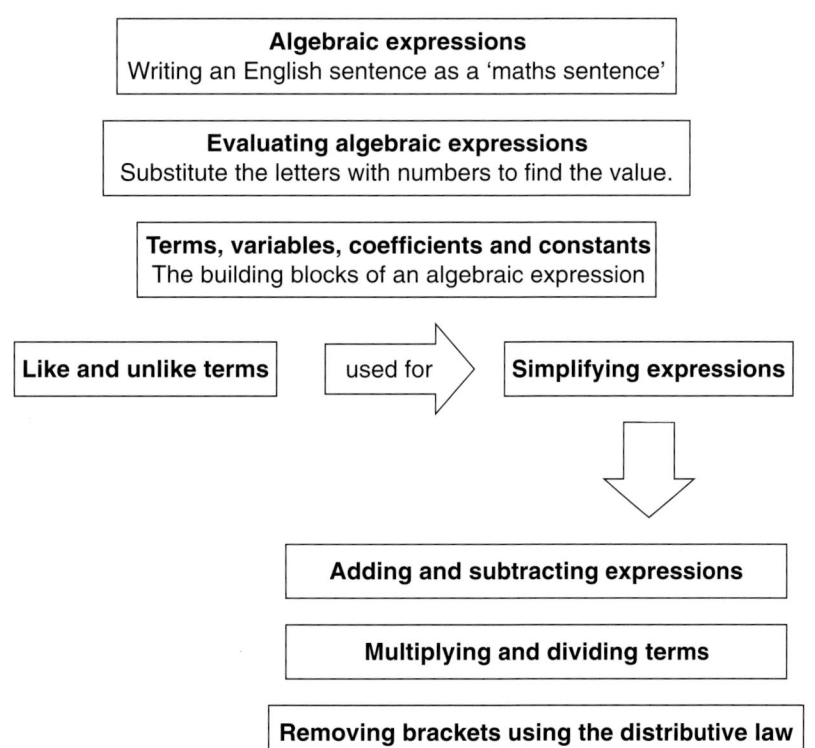

Algebraic expressions
Writing an English sentence as a 'maths sentence'

Evaluating algebraic expressions
Substitute the letters with numbers to find the value.

Terms, variables, coefficients and constants
The building blocks of an algebraic expression

Like and unlike terms   used for ➤   **Simplifying expressions**

Adding and subtracting expressions

Multiplying and dividing terms

Removing brackets using the distributive law

An introduction to geometry

After laying the foundation in Unit 8 by introducing measurement, it is now time to introduce the first elements of geometry.

Geometry is all about accuracy. The pencils the pupils use for drawing must be sharp. It is also vital that you show them good techniques for using a protractor, a pair of compasses and even a ruler precisely and accurately. There is a reason for every mark we make in geometric constructions, and if one of them is not accurate, the whole construction will be wrong.

We use the laws of geometry to progress from what we know for sure to find the size of an unknown angle, the length of a line segment, and so on. In geometry we cannot guess at anything – we can only use the information we are given and the rules of geometry to work out a new piece of information. Pupils need to be very careful not to assume something just because it 'looks' like it is true in the drawing. It is very important that they understand the difference between a rough sketch and an accurate construction.

Equipment

It would be useful to have the following equipment available, for use with your chalkboard or whiteboard.

- Large-sized ruler.
- Large-sized pair of compasses.
- Large-sized protractor.

Pupils will need card and a paper fastener for the activity on page 191 of the Coursebook.

Key vocabulary

3-dimensional	perpendicular
acute angle	perpendicular bisector
adjacent angle	plane
angle	point
arc	protractor
bisector	ray
complement	rectangle
complementary angles	reflex angle
construction	right angle
degree	rotation
depth	ruler
full circle	scale
full turn	square
geometry	straight angle
horizontal	supplement
length	supplementary angles
line	symbol
line segment	triangle
major angle	vertex
mid point	vertical
minor angle	vertically opposite angles
obtuse angle	width
pair of compasses	
pair of dividers	

Teaching and learning objectives

After studying the work covered in this unit, pupils should be able to

- represent and name points, lines, rays, line segments and planes correctly
- draw and name angles
- distinguish between the different types of angles
- measure and draw angles of different sizes accurately
- identify complementary, supplementary and vertically opposite angles and use them to find the size of unknown angles
- use the property of angles at a point to find the size of unknown angles
- draw an accurate geometric construction of an angle bisector, a perpendicular bisector of a line segment, a perpendicular to or from any point on a line segment and a 60° angle, and use these to construct simple geometric shapes.

Teaching hours

You should aim to devote approximately 10% of your total annual teaching hours to this unit.

The journey through Unit 10

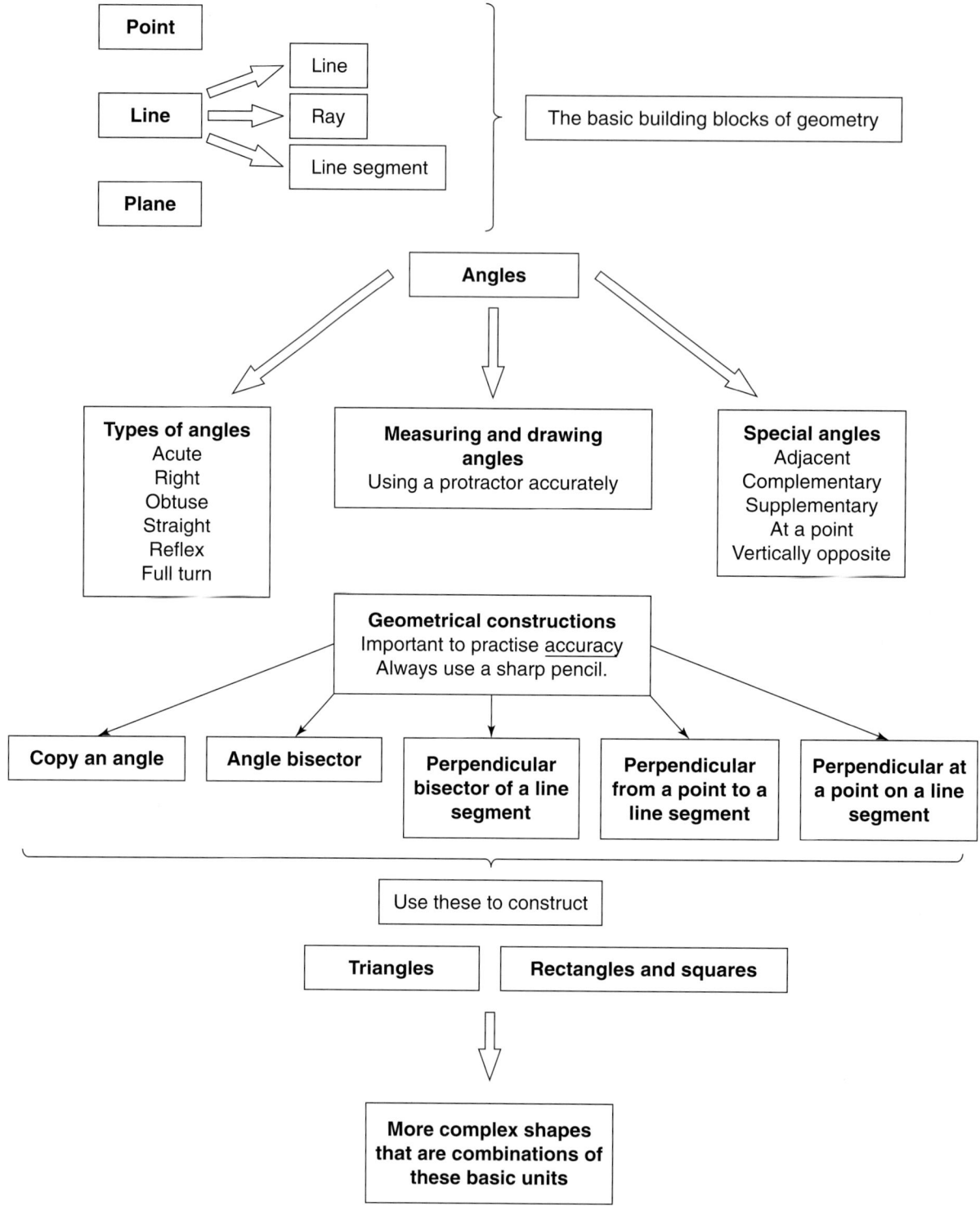

An introduction to coordinate geometry

The purpose of this unit is to introduce pupils to the rules and vocabulary used when plotting a graph. This will prepare them for later units containing more detailed work on some important types of graphs, such as the straight lines and parabolas.

For now it is important that pupils become experienced at plotting coordinates on a set of axes – and remembering which coordinate is x and which is y.

Equipment

As well as a chalkboard or whiteboard to write on, it would be useful to have the following equipment available.

- Large-sized ruler that you can use with your chalk/whiteboard.
- Large-sized set of compasses suitable for use with your chalk/whiteboard.
- Large-sized protractor that you can use with your chalk/whiteboard.
- Separate board that is prepared with a permanent grid for drawing graphs.

Pupils will need a supply of graph paper. The grid on page 23 can be photocopied for this purpose.

Teaching and learning objectives

After studying the work covered in this unit, pupils should be able to

- understand directed numbers and the Cartesian plane
- use an ordered pair to write down the coordinates of a point marked on a Cartesian plane
- locate and mark a point with given coordinates on a Cartesian plane
- plot a graph from a given set of points.

Teaching hours

You should aim to devote approximately 5% of your total annual teaching hours to this unit.

Key vocabulary

axis	origin (O)
Cartesian plane	plot
coordinates	quadrant
directed number	vertical
graph	x-axis
horizontal	x-coordinate
intersect	y-axis
ordered pair	y-coordinate

The journey through Unit 11

A grid of squares
A grid of squares + a rule = the start of coordinate geometry

Directed numbers
How far?
+
In what direction?

Positive numbers
Right →
or Up ↑

Negative numbers
Left ←
or Down ↓

Axes
Number lines at
right angles

Horizontal = x-**axis**
Vertical = y-**axis**
Intersect at the **origin**

together
they make

The Cartesian plane
(divided into four
quadrants)

Ordered pairs
(x-coordinate, y-coordinate)
Used to find and place any point on the
Cartesian plane

Plotting points (using coordinates) on a Cartesian plane makes a **graph**

© Hodder Education 2008 International Mathematics Teacher's Guide 1

Answers to the Coursebook

Unit 1 Integers

Exercise 1

1. a) 396   b) 5010
    c) 70 200   d) 9 002 051
    e) 762 504 019   f) 20 202 020
    g) 25 463   h) 370 000
    i) 1 000 204   j) 1240
    k) 633   l) 17 918
2. a) eighty-four
    b) twenty-three thousand, five hundred and ninety
    c) ninety-three million, one hundred and forty-five thousand, six hundred and seventy
    d) seven hundred and sixty-four thousand, eight hundred and nine
    e) six thousand, and forty-nine
    f) nine million, eighty thousand and four
3. a) 30
    b) 3 000 000
    c) 600
    d) 2000
    e) 4000
    f) 6
    g) 6000, 70
    h) 10 000, 20
    i) 500 000, 6000
    j) 40 000, 200
    k) 700 000, 5000
    l) 1 000 000 000, 6 000 000

Exercise 2

1. a) 203   b) 28
2. 26, 28, 30, 32, 34
3. 85, 87, 89, 91, 93, 95, 97, 99
4. a) 39, 74, 168, 421
    b) 3801, 3842, 3874, 4765, 5814
5. a) 429, 425, 399, 103, 84
    b) 9951, 9653, 9646, 9434
6. a) 76 541   b) 14 567
7. a) 9654   b) 4569
8. a) 8543, 8534, 8453, 8435, 8354, 8345, 5843, 5834, 5483, 5438, 5384, 5348, 4853, 4835, 4583, 4538, 4385, 4358, 3854, 3845, 3584, 3548, 3485, 3458
    b) reverse order of a)
    c) 6

Exercise 3

1. a) 29   b) 31
    c) 43   d) 43
    e) 53   f) 46
2. a) 91   b) 4
    c) 55   d) 63
    e) 38   f) 17
3. a) 788   b) 83
    c) 174   d) 952
    e) 2002   f) 12 203
    g) 201   h) 1735
    i) 1541   j) 1 000 000
    k) 3451   l) 15 455
4. a) 27   b) 56
    c) 35   d) 54
    e) 74   f) 70
    g) 120   h) 112
5. a) 5, 6, 3   b) 6, 9, 7, 2
    c) 9, 2, 3, 8, 1   d) 4, 4, 3, 2
6. 112 miles
7. £539
8. £276
9. a) 141 pupils
    b) 132 pupils
    c) 133 pupils
    d) 406 pupils
10. a) 1378 tickets
    b) 2269 tickets
11. 81 030 supporters

Exercise 4

1 a) 28   b) 46
c) 25   d) 35
2 a) 5   b) 92
c) 43   d) 68
e) 76   f) 17
g) 59   h) 21
3 a) 16   b) 17
c) 50   d) 49
e) 90   f) 105
g) 150   h) 301
i) 575   j) 4
4 a) 354   b) 428
c) 1284   d) 158
e) 2224   f) 469
g) 6268   h) 3277
i) 58 257   j) 2368

5 a)
```
    2  8  4
 -  1  9  6
    ───────
       8  8
```

b)
```
    7  2  2
 -  2  3  9
    ───────
    4  8  3
```

c)
```
 1  5  9  4
 -  9  0  6
 ──────────
    6  8  8
```

d)
```
 5  5  3  2  1
 -  5  4  0  3
 ─────────────
 4  9  9  1  8
```

6 89 spaces
7 384 boys
8 Car C
9 a) $74 more
b) $60 more

Exercise 5

1 a) 84   b) 85
c) 252   d) 549
e) 2112   f) 15 895
g) 24 072   h) 42 084
2 a) 1320   b) 12 300
c) 47 000   d) 38 400
3 a) 2310   b) 514
c) 100
4 40 doughnuts
5 a) 240 biscuits
b) $3.90
6 a) 210 chairs
b) 140 tables
c) 350 pencils
d) 280 rulers
7 a) 300 seconds
b) 420 seconds
c) 1200 seconds
d) 7200 seconds
8 960 pupils
9 10 000 m
10 a) 7590   b) 7140
c) 21 480   d) 12 300
e) 13 020   f) 21 510
g) 32 960   h) 9940
i) 18 960   j) 13 000
k) 15 180   l) 543 600

Exercise 6

1 a) 17   b) 157
c) 136   d) 75 rem 5
e) 393 rem 2   f) 206
g) 1098   h) 20 140
2 a) 4560   b) 465
c) 64   d) 654
e) 12 300   f) 170
3 a) 100   b) 702 000
c) 10
4 a) 253   b) 79
c) 537   d) 126
e) 45   f) 613
g) 26   h) 293
i) 412
5 a) 20 pencils
b) 16 erasers
c) 8 rulers
6 8 minibuses
7 15 notes
8 12 buses
9 5 lessons
10 7 minutes

Exercise 7

1
a) 1344
b) 2432
c) 4862
d) 11 130
e) 38 772
f) 76 812
g) 345 015
h) 6 620 544

2
a) 463
b) 158
c) 123
d) 256
e) 504
f) 654
g) 406
h) 208
i) 1520 rem 17
j) 115 rem 1
k) 1715 rem 137
l) 150 rem 28

3 £1392

4 1416 passengers

5
a) $2086
b) $2898
c) $9659

6
a) 16 rem 10
b) 25 rem 7
c) 17 rem 35
d) 14 rem 7

7
a) $8\frac{1}{2}$ litres
b) 7¢ change

8
a) 41 full boxes
b) 16 tins

Exercise 8

1
a) × ×
b) + +
c) + +
d) × ×
e) × ×
f) + +

2
a) 9
b) 3, 6
c) 13
d) 8
e) 15
f) 4, 13

Exercise 9

1
a) 37
b) 3
c) 9
d) 58
e) 6
f) 30
g) 5
h) 19
i) 14
j) 20
k) 24
l) 4
m) 0
n) 56
o) 56

2
a) × +
b) + ×
c) + ×
d) × +
e) × −
f) ÷ +
g) − ÷
h) ÷ + ×
i) × + ×

3
a) =
b) >
c) <
d) >
e) >
f) =
g) <
h) >
i) <
j) <

4
a) $14 - (8 - 3) = 9$
b) $2 \times (7 + 8) = 30$
c) $2 \times (7 + 3 \times 3) = 32$
d) $2 \times (7 + 3) \times 3 = 60$
e) $(2 \times 7 + 3) \times 3 = 51$
f) $4 \times (7 - 3) \times 5 = 80$

5
a) 5
b) 420
c) 20
d) 20
e) 8
f) 631
g) 324
h) 209

6 Many different answers are possible. Here is one example for each part.
a) $6 - 3 \times 2 + 1 = 1$
b) $6 - 3 - 2 + 1 = 2$
c) $(6 + 3) \div (2 + 1) = 3$
d) $6 - 3 + 2 - 1 = 4$
e) $6 \div 3 + 2 + 1 = 5$
f) $6 + 3 - 2 - 1 = 6$
g) $6 + 3 - 2 \times 1 = 7$
h) $6 \times 3 \div 2 - 1 = 8$
i) $6 \times 3 \div 2 \times 1 = 9$
j) $6 + 3 + 2 - 1 = 10$

7 25 more chairs

8
a) 63 children
b) 75 people

Exercise 10

1
a) warmer
b) colder
c) warmer
d) colder

2
a) less
b) more
c) less
d) more

3
a) Colombo
b) Moscow
c) $-22\,°C$, $-17\,°C$, $-7\,°C$, $0\,°C$, $3\,°C$, $15\,°C$, $21\,°C$

4 See number lines below.

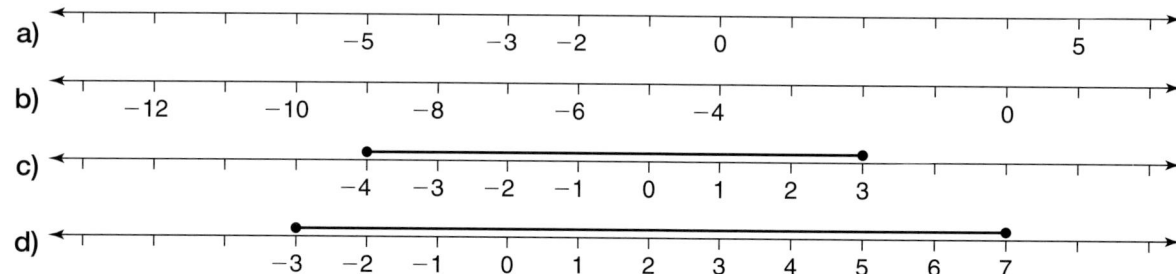

Exercise 11

1 a) -5 b) -5
  c) -7 d) -6
  e) 8 f) -9
  g) 3 h) -1
  i) -1 j) -4
  k) 4 l) -1
2 a) -11 b) -16
  c) -14 d) 20
  e) -21 f) -20
  g) -62 h) -129
3 a) 8 b) 8
  c) 7 d) 11
  e) -15 f) -26
  g) -41 h) -15
  i) -99
4 a) -9 b) -14
  c) 25 d) 13
  e) -35 f) 56
  g) -153 h) 26
5 a) 60 b) -120
  c) -70 d) -300
  e) -50 f) -130
  g) 240 h) -250
6 $6\,°C$
7 a) 13 b) 6
  c) 7 d) -1
  e) 7 f) 5
  g) -12 h) 13
  i) -11 j) 11
  k) 9 l) 0
  m) 5 n) 3
  o) 3 p) -7
  q) -6 r) -1
  s) 6 t) -8
  u) -28 v) 0
  w) -35 x) 19
8 a) 7 b) -1
  c) 36 d) -6
  e) 38 f) 15
  g) -15 h) 25
  i) 15 j) -6
  k) -26 l) -39
  m) -25 n) -416
  o) -9 p) 134
  q) -30 r) -158
  s) -50 t) 103
9 a) $3\,°C$ b) $10\,°C$
  c) $5\,°C$ d) $6\,°C$
  e) $-37\,°C$
10 $-15\,°C$

Exercise 12

1 a) 35 b) -35
  c) 35 d) 10
  e) -10 f) 10
  g) 1 h) -24
  i) -24 j) -45
  k) 64 l) -42
  m) 42 n) -80
  o) -80 p) 32
  q) -20 r) 60
  s) -30 t) 60
  u) -60 v) -100
  w) 216 x) 0
  y) -3360
2 a) -4 b) 4
  c) 5 d) -5
  e) -5 f) 5
  g) -6 h) -6
  i) 4 j) -8
  k) 6 l) -5
  m) -6 n) -59
  o) -13 p) -256
3 a) -6 b) 3
  c) -8 d) 9
  e) -10 f) -6
  g) 7 h) -6
  i) -22 j) 45
  k) -20 l) -71
  m) -187 n) 68

Unit 2 Factors and multiples

Exercise 1

1 a) $1 \times 18 = 18$; $2 \times 9 = 18$; $3 \times 6 = 18$
   b) 1, 2, 3, 6, 9, 18
2 a) $1 \times 20 = 20$; $2 \times 10 = 20$; $4 \times 5 = 20$
   b) 1, 2, 4, 5, 10, 20
3 a) 1, 2, 4, 8, 16
   b) 1, 2, 4, 7, 14, 28
   c) 1, 2, 3, 4, 6, 9, 12, 18, 36
   d) 1, 3, 5, 9, 15, 45
   e) 1, 2, 3, 4, 6, 8, 12, 16, 24, 48
   f) 1, 2, 5, 10, 25, 50
   g) 1, 3, 41, 123
   h) 1, 2, 3, 4, 6, 8, 9, 12, 16, 18, 24, 36, 48, 72, 144
4 a) 1, 2   b) 1, 3
   c) 1, 5   d) 1, 7
   e) 1, 11   f) 1, 13
   g) Many answers are possible.
      Two examples are 17 and 19.
5 a) 1, 2, 4   b) 1, 3, 9
   c) 1, 5, 25   d) 1, 7, 49
   e) Many answers are possible.
      Two examples are 121 and 169.
6 a) 1, 2, 3, 6   b) 1, 2, 5, 10
   c) 1, 2, 7, 14   d) 1, 2, 13, 26
   e) Many answers are possible.
      Two examples are 34 and 38.
7 a) no   b) yes
   c) no   d) yes
   e) yes   f) yes
8 a) yes   b) yes
   c) yes   d) yes
   e) no   f) yes
   g) no   h) yes
   i) no   j) yes
   k) yes   l) yes
9 a) 3, 6, 9, 12, 15
   b) 7, 14, 21, 28, 35
   c) 20, 40, 60, 80, 100
   d) 12, 24, 36, 48, 60
10 a) 20   b) 70
   c) third   d) eleventh
   e) 5   f) 5
   g) second   h) second
   i) fifth   j) third

11 a)

×	2	3	6	7	9
2	E	E	E	E	E
3	E	O	E	O	O
6	E	E	E	E	E
7	E	O	E	O	O
9	E	O	E	O	O

b)

×	O	E
O	O	E
E	E	E

c) If the number is even all multiples are even.
   If the number is odd, there is an equal
   number of odd and even multiples.
12 a) 6, 12, 18, 36
   b) 5, 10, 15, 20, 30, 40, 60, 120
   c) 2, 4, 10, 20, 50, 100
   d) 4, 8, 12, 16, 24, 32, 48, 96

Exercise 2

1 a) divisible by 2, 3
   b) divisible by 3, 5
   c) none
   d) divisible by 2, 3
   e) divisible by 3
   f) divisible by 2
   g) divisible by 2
   h) divisible by 2, 5
2 a) divisible by 9
   b) divisible by 4, 9
   c) divisible by 4
   d) divisible by 9
   e) none
   f) divisible by 9
   g) divisible by 4, 9
   h) divisible by 4
3 a) yes   b) yes
   c) yes
4 a) yes   b) yes
   c) yes
   d) i) no   ii) yes
      iii) yes   iv) no

Exercise 3

1 2

2 3, 5, 7, 11, 13, 17, 19, 23, 29, 31, 37, 41, 43, 47, 53, 59, 61, 67, 71, 73, 79, 83, 89, 97

3 a) 101
   b) 997

4 5 and 7
   11 and 13
   17 and 19
   29 and 31
   41 and 43

5 a) Many different answers are possible.
      One example is 5 and 7.
   b) No, one of the numbers can never be 2.

6 a) yes
   b) yes
   c) no

7 Many different answers are possible.
   One example is 13 and 31.

8 a) $12 = 2 \times 2 \times 3$
   b) $20 = 2 \times 2 \times 5$
   c) $28 = 2 \times 2 \times 7$
   d) $45 = 3 \times 3 \times 5$
   e) $66 = 2 \times 3 \times 11$
   f) $108 = 2 \times 2 \times 3 \times 3 \times 3$
   g) $250 = 2 \times 5 \times 5 \times 5$
   h) $510 = 2 \times 3 \times 5 \times 17$
   i) $1089 = 3 \times 3 \times 11 \times 11$
   j) $902 = 2 \times 11 \times 41$
   k) $2028 = 2 \times 2 \times 3 \times 13 \times 13$
   l) $4725 = 3 \times 3 \times 3 \times 5 \times 5 \times 7$

9 a) 1000
   b) 1 000 000
   c) 2700
   d) 56 250 000
   e) 3 294 225
   f) 926 859 375

Exercise 4

1 a) 6   b) 8
   c) 2   d) 4
   e) 11   f) 4
   g) 3   h) 15
   i) 18   j) 108
   k) 675   l) 12
   m) 45   n) 54
   o) 8   p) 14
   q) 180   r) 350

2 a) 24   b) 160
   c) 20   d) 180
   e) 90   f) 24
   g) 40   h) 630
   i) 4800   j) 5880
   k) 7956   l) 2940
   m) 9408   n) 2 835 000
   o) 138 600

3 a) $108 = 2^2 \times 3^3$
   b) $162 = 2 \times 3^4$
   c) $2 \times 3^3 = 54$
   d) $2^2 \times 3^4 = 324$

4 a) $216 = 2^3 \times 3^3$
   b) $288 = 2^5 \times 3^2$
   c) $2^3 \times 3^2 = 72$
   d) $2^5 \times 3^3 = 864$

5 9.18 a.m.

6 24 m

7 367

8 24

9 185

10 36

Unit 3 Fractions

Exercise 1

1 a) $\frac{3}{4}$ b) $\frac{1}{6}$
   c) $\frac{3}{7}$ d) $\frac{5}{8}$
   e) $\frac{7}{9}$ f) $\frac{1}{10}$
   g) $\frac{6}{11}$ h) $\frac{11}{12}$
   i) $\frac{9}{20}$

2 a) one-quarter
   b) five-sixths
   c) one-third
   d) three-eighths
   e) five-ninths
   f) nine-tenths
   g) six-sevenths
   h) seven-twelfths
   i) eleven-twentieths

3 a) $\frac{4}{9}$ b) $\frac{2}{8}$
   c) $\frac{8}{16}$ d) $\frac{3}{12}$
   e) $\frac{7}{10}$ f) $\frac{2}{4}$
   g) $\frac{5}{100}$ h) $\frac{4}{9}$

4 a) improper fraction
   b) proper fraction
   c) proper fraction
   d) improper fraction
   e) improper fraction
   f) mixed number
   g) improper fraction
   h) improper fraction
   i) mixed number

5 a) $1\frac{3}{10}$ b) $1\frac{1}{2}$
   c) $2\frac{1}{8}$ d) $3\frac{3}{4}$
   e) $4\frac{3}{5}$ f) $4\frac{6}{7}$
   g) $2\frac{9}{11}$ h) $4\frac{3}{10}$
   i) $3\frac{1}{9}$

6 a) $\frac{27}{10}$ b) $\frac{8}{5}$
   c) $\frac{35}{6}$ d) $\frac{63}{20}$
   e) $\frac{41}{9}$ f) $\frac{53}{7}$
   g) $\frac{23}{2}$ h) $\frac{19}{4}$

7 $\frac{2}{8}$

8 $\frac{3}{12}$

Exercise 2

1 a) $\frac{9}{18}$ b) $\frac{16}{24}$ c) $\frac{30}{24}$
   d) $\frac{49}{35}$ e) $\frac{15}{18}$ f) $\frac{12}{28}$
   g) $\frac{22}{16}$ h) $\frac{100}{90}$ i) $\frac{63}{90}$
   j) $\frac{15}{36}$ k) $\frac{33}{176}$ l) $\frac{25}{45}$

2 a) 4 b) 9 c) 30
   d) 30 e) 56 f) 99
   g) 52 h) 135 i) 187
   j) 10 k) 3 l) 7

3 a) 4, 27 b) 14, 40 c) 33, 60
   d) 24, 85 e) 15, 72 f) 8, 16
   g) 12, 18, 30 h) 6, 32, 28

4 a) $\frac{2}{3}$ b) $\frac{4}{5}$ c) $\frac{3}{4}$
   d) $\frac{2}{7}$ e) $\frac{7}{8}$ f) $\frac{8}{9}$
   g) $\frac{2}{5}$ h) $\frac{6}{25}$ i) $\frac{4}{5}$
   j) $\frac{5}{6}$ k) $\frac{11}{12}$ l) $\frac{5}{13}$
   m) $\frac{2}{3}$ n) $\frac{1}{3}$ o) $\frac{6}{13}$
   p) $\frac{7}{25}$ q) $\frac{2}{7}$ r) $\frac{3}{7}$
   s) $\frac{5}{11}$ t) $\frac{5}{8}$ u) $\frac{7}{13}$

5 a) $\frac{1}{3}$ b) $\frac{1}{3}$
   c) $\frac{1}{3}$ d) $\frac{1}{2}$
   e) $\frac{1}{2}$

6 a) $1\frac{1}{2}$ b) $2\frac{2}{3}$
   c) $3\frac{1}{4}$ d) $4\frac{3}{5}$
   e) $5\frac{5}{6}$ f) $6\frac{6}{7}$
   g) $7\frac{3}{7}$ h) $8\frac{4}{5}$
   i) $9\frac{2}{9}$ j) $10\frac{11}{12}$

7 a) yes b) yes
   c) no d) yes
   e) yes f) no
   g) yes h) yes

8 a) $\frac{7}{10}$ b) $\frac{1}{5}$

9 a) 24 pupils b) $\frac{1}{6}$

Exercise 3

1 a) $\frac{3}{4}$ b) $\frac{2}{11}$ c) $\frac{22}{25}$

   d) $-\frac{17}{25}$ e) $\frac{11}{12}$ f) $-\frac{3}{16}$

2 a) $<$ b) $>$ c) $>$

   d) $<$ e) $>$ f) $>$

3 a) $\frac{2}{3} < \frac{3}{4} < \frac{7}{8}$

   b) $-\frac{1}{6} < \frac{3}{16} < \frac{5}{24}$

   c) $\frac{11}{20} < \frac{11}{18} < \frac{11}{12}$

   d) $\frac{13}{24} < \frac{5}{9} < \frac{16}{27}$

4 a) $\frac{4}{5} > \frac{3}{4} > \frac{7}{10}$

   b) $\frac{5}{8} > -\frac{1}{2} > -\frac{3}{5}$

   c) $\frac{2}{3} > \frac{3}{5} > \frac{4}{7}$

   d) $\frac{5}{6} > \frac{3}{4} > \frac{7}{10}$

Exercise 4

1 a) $\frac{3}{8}$ b) $\frac{7}{12}$ c) $\frac{7}{10}$

   d) $\frac{8}{15}$ e) $\frac{9}{14}$ f) $\frac{7}{24}$

2 a) $\frac{1}{8}$ b) $\frac{1}{12}$ c) $\frac{3}{10}$

   d) $\frac{2}{15}$ e) $\frac{5}{14}$ f) $\frac{1}{24}$

3 a) $1\frac{1}{4}$ b) $1\frac{1}{2}$ c) $1\frac{11}{20}$

   d) $1\frac{8}{21}$ e) $1\frac{5}{24}$ f) $1\frac{11}{18}$

4 a) $\frac{1}{8}$ b) $\frac{8}{15}$

   c) $\frac{5}{8}$ d) $\frac{17}{45}$

   e) $\frac{5}{24}$ f) $\frac{19}{48}$

5 a) $4\frac{1}{4}$ b) $3\frac{5}{6}$

   c) $4\frac{3}{8}$ d) $5\frac{17}{20}$

   e) $6\frac{13}{30}$ f) $5\frac{9}{20}$

6 a) $1\frac{1}{10}$ b) $\frac{5}{12}$

   c) $\frac{5}{8}$ d) $3\frac{3}{10}$

   e) $1\frac{27}{40}$ f) $\frac{47}{48}$

7 a) 1 b) $\frac{1}{8}$ c) $5\frac{1}{4}$

   d) $6\frac{23}{40}$ e) $7\frac{3}{4}$ f) $\frac{1}{18}$

   g) $\frac{5}{12}$ h) $4\frac{5}{8}$ i) $3\frac{1}{6}$

   j) $10\frac{17}{40}$ k) $1\frac{1}{12}$ l) $12\frac{5}{24}$

Exercise 5

1 a) $\frac{1}{6}$ b) $\frac{1}{20}$ c) $\frac{1}{10}$

   d) $\frac{5}{21}$ e) $\frac{1}{6}$ f) $\frac{1}{4}$

   g) $\frac{4}{5}$ h) $\frac{7}{16}$

2 a) $\frac{3}{8}$ b) $\frac{3}{10}$ c) $\frac{1}{3}$

   d) $\frac{1}{3}$ e) $\frac{3}{16}$ f) $\frac{2}{35}$

   g) $\frac{1}{2}$ h) $\frac{1}{4}$ i) $\frac{1}{6}$

   j) $\frac{1}{6}$ k) $\frac{1}{28}$ l) $\frac{1}{9}$

3 a) 2 b) $1\frac{1}{9}$ c) $2\frac{8}{9}$

   d) $\frac{1}{2}$

4 a) $1\frac{1}{8}$ b) 2 c) $3\frac{3}{4}$

   d) $3\frac{17}{20}$ e) $4\frac{7}{8}$ f) $1\frac{13}{15}$

   g) 14 h) $13\frac{1}{2}$ i) $2\frac{7}{10}$

   j) $8\frac{3}{4}$ k) $5\frac{7}{16}$ l) $8\frac{1}{18}$

5 a) $47\frac{2}{3}$ b) $\frac{1}{3}$

   c) $2\frac{11}{12}$ d) $\frac{17}{24}$

   e) 4 f) $12\frac{4}{5}$

6 a) $2\frac{3}{5}$ b) $3\frac{1}{2}$

   c) $5\frac{2}{5}$ d) $2\frac{1}{2}$

   e) $1\frac{1}{3}$ f) $3\frac{4}{7}$

   g) $\frac{2}{3}$ h) $1\frac{1}{3}$

7 a) $\frac{4}{5}$ b) $\frac{4}{15}$

   c) 15 sweets

Exercise 6

1 a) $\frac{1}{10}$ b) $\frac{3}{8}$ c) $\frac{1}{10}$

d) $\frac{1}{3}$ e) $\frac{4}{7}$ f) $\frac{4}{9}$

g) $\frac{4}{11}$ h) $\frac{9}{10}$

2 a) 2   b) $\frac{2}{5}$ c) $2\frac{5}{8}$

d) $3\frac{1}{3}$ e) 22   f) $7\frac{1}{3}$

g) $2\frac{8}{27}$ h) $3\frac{1}{2}$

3 a) $\frac{5}{6}$ b) $\frac{9}{16}$ c) $\frac{4}{5}$

d) $1\frac{1}{3}$ e) $\frac{2}{3}$ f) $1\frac{1}{2}$

g) $\frac{2}{3}$ h) $1\frac{1}{6}$ i) $1\frac{1}{2}$

j) $1\frac{4}{5}$ k) $1\frac{1}{14}$ l) $1\frac{3}{4}$

4 a) $\frac{2}{3}$ b) $1\frac{3}{8}$ c) $1\frac{1}{7}$

d) $4\frac{2}{3}$ e) $13\frac{1}{2}$ f) $\frac{4}{5}$

g) $1\frac{1}{2}$ h) $1\frac{1}{4}$ i) $2\frac{2}{7}$

j) $3\frac{6}{25}$ k) $1\frac{4}{5}$ l) $3\frac{1}{3}$

5 a) $1\frac{11}{25}$ b) $\frac{1}{4}$

c) 1   d) $\frac{3}{4}$

e) $5\frac{1}{3}$ f) $2\frac{19}{64}$

g) $1\frac{8}{27}$ h) $7\frac{7}{15}$

i) $\frac{5}{21}$ j) $\frac{35}{36}$

k) $\frac{7}{45}$ l) $11\frac{3}{7}$

m) $\frac{7}{72}$ n) $\frac{14}{25}$

o) $\frac{25}{126}$

6 a) 21 books   b) 23 videos

7 $\frac{32}{45}$

8 $2\frac{2}{5}$

9 $\frac{16}{21}$

Exercise 7

1 a) $\frac{5}{12}$ b) $1\frac{1}{12}$

c) $\frac{7}{12}$ d) $2\frac{1}{12}$

e) $2\frac{1}{4}$ f) $1\frac{5}{6}$

g) $-\frac{1}{12}$ h) $\frac{7}{24}$

i) $\frac{19}{24}$ j) $\frac{19}{20}$

k) 6   l) $-2\frac{1}{3}$

2 a) $\frac{3}{8}$ b) $1\frac{3}{4}$

c) $\frac{3}{10}$ d) $\frac{13}{25}$

e) $\frac{7}{17}$ f) $\frac{9}{20}$

g) $3\frac{2}{3}$ h) $4\frac{1}{4}$

i) $\frac{11}{20}$ j) 3

k) $1\frac{1}{4}$ l) $1\frac{1}{12}$

m) $1\frac{32}{35}$ n) $11\frac{11}{14}$

Exercise 8

1 a) $\frac{1}{4}$ b) $\frac{1}{3}$

c) $\frac{3}{5}$ d) $\frac{4}{25}$

e) $\frac{7}{30}$ f) $\frac{1}{13}$

2 a) 9 hours
b) 8 months
c) $18\frac{3}{4}$ seconds
d) $6\frac{6}{7}$ days
e) 2700 seconds
f) 78 weeks

3 $8

4 98 km

5 $3.20

6 $\frac{1}{3}$

7 $\frac{1}{4}$

8 $12.80

9 $2\frac{1}{2}$ metres

10 216 hectares

11 $5.00

12 189 chairs

Unit 4 Decimals

Exercise 1

1 a) $\frac{3}{100}$ b) $\frac{7}{10\,000}$

c) $\frac{6}{1000}$ d) $\frac{2}{10}$

e) $\frac{5}{100\,000}$ f) $\frac{6}{10\,000}$

g) $6, \frac{7}{100}$ h) $10, \frac{8}{10}$

i) $2000, \frac{2}{1000}$ j) $10, \frac{4}{100\,000}$

k) $\frac{6}{1000}, \frac{3}{1\,000\,000}$ l) $200, \frac{4}{100\,000\,000}$

2 a) 3   b) 6
c) 4   d) 2
e) 5   f) 4
g) 1   h) 2
i) 3   j) 6
k) 7   l) 8

3 a) $(5 \times 100) + (6 \times 10) + (7 \times 1)$

b) 6042

c) $(8 \times 1) + \left(3 \times \frac{1}{10}\right)$

d) 2.07

e) $(1 \times 10) + (9 \times 1) + \left(2 \times \frac{1}{100}\right)$

f) 0.045

g) $\left(2 \times \frac{1}{100}\right) + \left(8 \times \frac{1}{1000}\right)$

h) $(9 \times 10) + \left(3 \times \frac{1}{100}\right) + \left(2 \times \frac{1}{1000}\right)$

i) $(9 \times 1) + \left(8 \times \frac{1}{10}\right) + \left(7 \times \frac{1}{100}\right)$

j) $(1 \times 1) + \left(2 \times \frac{1}{10}\right) + \left(3 \times \frac{1}{100}\right)$

$+ \left(4 \times \frac{1}{1000}\right) + \left(5 \times \frac{1}{10\,000}\right)$

4 a) 0.6   b) 0.02   c) 0.008
d) 0.26   e) 0.081   f) 6.9
g) 5.02   h) 11.007   i) 18.06
j) 56.39   k) 200.057   l) 500.203
m) 70.405   n) 613.7008

5 a) 0.5, 0.6, 0.7, 0.8
b) 0.07, 0.08, 0.09, 0.1
c) 0.86, 0.87, 0.88, 0.89
d) 0.24, 0.25, 0.26, 0.27
e) 0.62, 0.64, 0.66, 0.68
f) 0.184, 0.186, 0.188, 0.19
g) 0.37, 0.39, 0.41, 0.43
h) 0.823, 0.826, 0.829, 0.832
i) 0.957, 0.961, 0.965, 0.969
j) 0.11, 0.1105, 0.111, 0.1115

6 a) A = 10.5, B = 11
b) C = 5.2, D = 5.6
c) E = 0.54, F = 0.59
d) G = 0.751, H = 0.757

Exercise 2

1 a) 0.45   b) 0.374   c) 0.4059
d) −0.27   e) 0.042   f) 0.6173
g) −0.349   h) 0.08   i) −0.349

2 a) >   b) >   c) <
d) >   e) >   f) >
g) >   h) <   i) >
j) <   k) >   l) >

3 a) 3.001, 3.01, 3.1, 3.15, 3.2
b) 3.567, 3.576, 3.657, 3.675
c) 0.1, 0.15, 0.45, 0.5, 0.55
d) 2.914, 2.93, 2.939, 2.941

4 a) 9.87, 9.78, 8.97, 8.79
b) 1.5, 0.15, 0.015, 0.000 15
c) 2.701, 2.7, 2.67, 2.599
d) 1.999, 1.993, 1.939, 1.909
e) 2.202, 2.201, 2.102, 2.012

5 See number lines below.

a) 2.1   2.4   2.55   2.7

b) 3.03   3.07   3.12   3.16

c) 0.02   0.035   0.065   0.08

d) 1.22   1.25   1.28   1.31   1.345   1.38

6 151.34 cm, 151.54 cm, 152.34 cm, 152.45 cm

7 a) Pineapple C   b) Pineapple A

Exercise 3

1 a) 8.86   b) 12.449
   c) 17.49   d) 96.325
   e) 7.56   f) 14.545
2 a) 6.23   b) 24.32
   c) 24.68   d) 2.886
   e) 2.927   f) 15.927
3 a) 10.9   b) 1.65
   c) 0.9   d) 11
   e) 1.2   f) 0.6
   g) 0.24   h) 8.9
4 a) 6.84   b) 86.33
   c) 5.22   d) 5.003
   e) 3   f) 1.2364
   g) 15.781   h) 8.28
   i) 17.803   j) 6.273
   k) 55.411   l) 28.89
5 a) i) $3.30   ii) $1.70
   b) i) $11.24   ii) $3.76
   c) i) 83¢   ii) $9.17
   d) i) $16.24   ii) $33.76
6 4.35 kg
7 4.88 m
8 1.55 m
9 $82.69
10 0.719 seconds
11 7.61 mm

Exercise 4

1 a) 250.6   b) 2506
   c) 25060   d) 9.3
   e) 93   f) 930
   g) 0.623   h) 6.23
   i) 62.3   j) 94.51
   k) 945.1   l) 9451
2 a) 3.77   b) 0.377
   c) 0.0377   d) 0.027
   e) 0.0027   f) 0.00027
   g) 18.902   h) 1.8902
   i) 0.18902   j) 0.9
   k) 0.09   l) 0.009
3 a) i) 0.64   ii) 6.4
     iii) 64
   b) i) 0.64   ii) 0.064
     iii) 0.0064
4 a) €13.50   b) €135.00
   c) €1350.00
5 a) £2.50   b) £25.00
   c) £250.00
6 a) $7.95   b) 12¢ ($0.12)
   c) 66.9¢

Exercise 5

1 a) 8.5   b) 0.36
   c) 1.3   d) 0.048
   e) 0.006   f) 0.144
   g) 0.063   h) 0.64
2 a) 0.0007   b) 0.01
   c) 0.0001   d) 8.75
   e) 29.808   f) 54.53
   g) 1.03   h) 97.82
   i) 57.78   j) 0.0001776
   k) 144   l) 611.8
   m) 19.596   n) 56.43
   o) 5.74328   p) 8.9768
   q) 740.3   r) 48.19218
   s) 6.38   t) 376.8
3 a) 21¢ = $0.21   b) $1.84
   c) 78¢ = $0.78
4 a) $13.93   b) $10.08
   c) $54.21   d) $26.24
5 a) 260.5284 baht   b) 43.4214 baht
   c) 3922.3998 baht
6 a) $15.339   b) $1.5339
   c) $74.6498
7 a) £4.34   b) £5.12
   c) £2.60   d) £2.34

Exercise 6

1 a) 4   b) 15
   c) 15   d) 4
   e) 50
2 a) 1.75   b) 1.6
   c) 2.4   d) 1.75
   e) 1.125
3 a) 12.3   b) 2.92
   c) 6.05   d) 1430
   e) 0.05   f) 12.5
   g) 6.54   h) 37.5
4 a) 37   b) 5.6
   c) 43.75   d) 46.9
   e) 10.62   f) 34.2
   g) 30.588   h) 3.57
5 $0.668 = 66.8¢
6 $0.11 = 11¢
7 $3.60
8 $6.30
9 67 pieces
10 45 glasses

Exercise 7

1 a) $\frac{3}{10}$ b) $\frac{7}{10}$

c) $\frac{7}{100}$ d) $\frac{9}{100}$

e) $\frac{9}{1000}$ f) $\frac{3}{1000}$

g) $\frac{1}{2}$ h) $\frac{3}{5}$

i) $\frac{3}{25}$ j) $\frac{1}{4}$

k) $\frac{18}{25}$ l) $\frac{9}{25}$

m) $\frac{3}{40}$ n) $\frac{9}{200}$

o) $\frac{12}{25}$ p) $\frac{9}{50}$

2 a) 0.19 b) 0.023
c) 0.2 d) 0.8
e) 1.75 f) 0.75
g) 0.625 h) 0.125
i) 0.35 j) 0.95

3 a) $1\frac{3}{5}$ b) $1\frac{2}{5}$

c) $5\frac{1}{500}$ d) $4\frac{1}{200}$

e) $12\frac{3}{20}$ f) $24\frac{7}{20}$

g) $20\frac{3}{125}$ h) $50\frac{21}{250}$

4 a) 2.3 b) 5.7
c) 1.08 d) 2.04
e) 6.25 f) 4.75
g) 3.375 h) 7.875
i) 1.3125 j) 3.1875

Exercise 8

1 a) $0.\dot{7}$ b) $0.\dot{1}$

c) $0.\dot{3}\dot{6}$ d) $0.\dot{8}\dot{2}$

e) $0.\dot{1}3\dot{5}$ f) $0.\dot{2}1\dot{6}$

g) $0.1\dot{6}$ h) $0.\dot{8}6\dot{1}$

i) $0.\dot{7}\dot{2}$ j) $0.\dot{1}23\dot{4}$

k) $0.\dot{5}857\,14\dot{2}$

2 a) $0.\dot{8}$ b) $0.\dot{4}$

c) $0.\dot{5}\dot{1}$ d) $0.\dot{7}\dot{2}$

e) $0.\dot{1}4285\dot{7}$ f) $0.\dot{8}5714\dot{2}$

g) $0.0\dot{3}$ h) $0.4\dot{6}$

i) $0.8\dot{3}$ j) $0.\dot{7}\dot{2}$

Unit 5 Power numbers

Exercise 1

1 a) 4^4
b) 3^8
c) 8^7
d) $(0.3)^3$
e) $(1.6)^5$
f) 12^7

2

Number	Index form	Value
$10 \times 10 \times 10 \times 10 \times 10 \times 10$	10^6	1 000 000
$10 \times 10 \times 10 \times 10 \times 10$	10^5	100 000
$10 \times 10 \times 10 \times 10$	10^4	10 000
$10 \times 10 \times 10$	10^3	1 000
10×10	10^2	100
10	10^1	10
1	10^0	1

3

Number	Index form	Value
$5 \times 5 \times 5 \times 5 \times 5 \times 5$	5^6	15 625
$5 \times 5 \times 5 \times 5 \times 5$	5^5	3 125
$5 \times 5 \times 5 \times 5$	5^4	625
$5 \times 5 \times 5$	5^3	125
5×5	5^2	25
5	5^1	5
1	5^0	1

Number	Index form	Value
$4 \times 4 \times 4 \times 4 \times 4 \times 4$	4^6	4096
$4 \times 4 \times 4 \times 4 \times 4$	4^5	1024
$4 \times 4 \times 4 \times 4$	4^4	256
$4 \times 4 \times 4$	4^3	64
4×4	4^2	16
4	4^1	4
1	4^0	1

4 a) 8
b) 36
c) 81
d) 144
e) 625
f) 10 000 000

5 a) $2^2 \times 3^2$
b) $2^3 \times 3^2 \times 5$
c) $2 \times 3^3 \times 5$
d) $2 \times 3 \times 5^2$
e) $2^4 \times 3 \times 5^2$
f) $3^4 \times 5^2 \times 7$

Exercise 2

1 a) 2^7
b) 4^9
c) 6^3
d) 8^7
e) 9^0
f) 2^{-2}
g) 5^{-2}
h) 3^{-1}
i) 8^{-5}

2 a) 2^3
b) 4^2
c) 6^1
d) 8^1
e) 3^6
f) 2^{-4}
g) 5^{12}
h) 11^{-5}
i) 7^{-1}

3 a) 8^2
b) 7^{-5}
c) $(2.5)^{-1}$
d) $4^0 = 1$
e) 10^{-1}
f) 6^6
g) $(0.1)^{-12}$
h) 5^{-15}
i) 4^5

4 a) $4^2 \times 8^7$
b) 4×5^{-2}
c) $2^{-2} \times 5^5$
d) $3^{-3} \times 8^4$
e) $3^4 \times 7^2 \times 10^1$

5 a) 2^3
b) 3^1
c) $2^{-4} \times 5^3$

Exercise 3

1

Ordinary number	Working out	Standard form
300 000	$3 \times 100\,000$	3×10^5
75 000	$7.5 \times 10\,000$	7.5×10^4
800 000 000	$8 \times 100\,000\,000$	8×10^8
35 000 000 000 000	$3.5 \times 10\,000\,000\,000\,000$	3.5×10^{13}
62 300 000 000 000	$6.23 \times 10\,000\,000\,000\,000$	6.23×10^{13}
5 400 000 000	$5.4 \times 1\,000\,000\,000$	5.4×10^9
69 300 000	$6.93 \times 10\,000\,000$	6.93×10^7
453 100 000 000	$4.531 \times 100\,000\,000\,000$	4.531×10^{11}
697 000	$6.97 \times 100\,000$	6.97×10^5
453 120	$4.5312 \times 100\,000$	4.5312×10^5
109 700	$1\,097 \times 100\,000$	1.097×10^5

2 a) -1
b) -5
c) -9
d) -3
e) -11
f) -13

3

Ordinary number	Working out	Standard form
0.000 03	$3 \times 0.000\,01$	3×10^{-5}
0.007 5	7.5×0.001	7.5×10^{-3}
0.000 008 75	$8.75 \times 0.000\,001$	8.75×10^{-6}
0.000 000 003 5	$3.5 \times 0.000\,000\,001$	3.5×10^{-9}
0.000 000 000 006 23	$6.23 \times 0.000\,000\,000\,001$	6.23×10^{-12}
0.000 000 5	$5 \times 0.000\,000\,1$	5×10^{-7}
0.000 000 047 25	$4.725 \times 0.000\,000\,01$	4.725×10^{-8}
0.05	5×0.01	5×10^{-2}
0.000 007 85	$7.85 \times 0.000\,001$	7.85×10^{-6}

4 a) 3×10^{11}
b) 8×10^{7}
c) 7×10^{8}
d) 2×10^{9}
e) 4.2×10^{7}
f) 2.1×10^{10}
g) 3.7×10^{9}
h) 6.3×10^{2}
i) 3.219×10^{9}
j) 6.5412×10^{8}
k) 8.97213×10^{5}
l) 4.267×10^{10}

5 a) 3×10^{-3} b) 2.3×10^{-9}
c) 8×10^{-4} d) 7.395×10^{-8}
e) 4×10^{-2} f) 4.5×10^{-8}
g) 2.34×10^{-2} h) 2.34×10^{-9}
i) 6.7×10^{-3} j) 5×10^{-9}
k) 3×10^{-1} l) 3.4×10^{-13}

6 a) 600 000
b) 2000
c) 50 000 000
d) 900 000 000
e) 3 700 000 000
f) 28
g) 99 000 000 000
h) 71 000
i) 397
j) 817.2
k) 7 431 200
l) 1 234 000 000

7 a) 0.35
b) 0.000 5
c) 0.000 072
d) 0.0061
e) 0.000 000 000 117
f) 0.000 000 813 5
g) 0.064 62
h) 0.000 000 004 001
i) 0.000 005 5
j) 0.000 000 065
k) 0.000 000 000 031 67
l) 0.000 014 12

8 a) 2.4×10^{3}
b) 4.2×10^{-8}
c) $5 \times 10 = 50$

9 2.088×10^{9} cans

10 $1.525\ 965 \times 10^{16}$ km

11 Pluto < Saturn < Jupiter

12 9×10^{-28} g

Unit 6 Other number systems
Exercise 1

1 a) 12
b) 29
c) 41
d) 77
e) 95
f) 104
g) 340
h) 416
i) 768
j) 1684
k) 2436

2 a) XXV
b) LII
c) LXVIII
d) XCIX
e) CXLVI
f) DLV
g) CMXLI
h) MXXXIII
i) MCMXXXIX
j) MCMXCII
k) MMDXXXVII

3 a) pack of 12 toilet rolls
b) 6 apples
c) breakfast cereal (500 grams)
d) orange squash (750 millilitres)
e) 320 grams of cheese
f) roll of 24 black rubbish bags
g) 8 slices of bacon
h) pack of 5 180-minute videotapes
i) 1500 gram tub of ice cream
j) 240 tea bags

Unit 7 Approximation and estimation

Exercise 1

1 **a)** 4870 **b)** 4900
c) 5000
2 **a)** 7430 **b)** 7400
c) 7000
3 **a)** **i)** 7610 **ii)** 7600
iii) 8000
b) **i)** 980 **ii)** 1000
iii) 1000
c) **i)** 61 120 **ii)** 61 100
iii) 61 000
d) **i)** 9710 **ii)** 9700
iii) 10 000
e) **i)** 620 **ii)** 600
iii) 1000
f) **i)** 9950 **ii)** 9900
iii) 10 000
g) **i)** 5760 **ii)** 5800
iii) 6000
h) **i)** 7500 **ii)** 7500
iii) 8000
i) **i)** 7500 **ii)** 7500
iii) 8000
j) **i)** 7500 **ii)** 7500
iii) 7000

4 Different answers are possible. Here is one example for each part.
a) 19 000 people
b) 260 people
c) 140 marbles
d) $50
e) 230 pupils
f) 5 600 000
g) 500 00 km²
h) 11 000 km
i) €51
j) 700 pupils

5 Many different answers are possible. Choose one example from each range for the number x.
a) $745 \leqslant x \leqslant 749$
b) $750 \leqslant x \leqslant 754$
c) $8450 \leqslant x \leqslant 8499$
d) $8500 \leqslant x \leqslant 8549$

6 42 500 spectators
7 **a)** 135 postcards
b) 144 postcards
8 2749 tiles

Exercise 2

1 **a)** 3.962 **b)** 3.96
c) 4.0
2 **a)** 567.65 **b)** 567.7
c) 568
3 **a)** 2.4 **b)** 0.96
c) 0.97 **d)** 15.281
e) 0.06 **f)** 4.99
g) 5.00 **h)** 17.55
i) 17.555
4 **a)** 4.83 **b)** 1.64
c) 6.98 **d)** 2.89
e) 14.06 **f)** 28.07
g) 4.83 **h)** 2.84
i) 7.08 **j)** 17.04
k) 0.99 **l)** 0.28
5 **a)** 4.9 **b)** 12.84
c) 0.048 **d)** 6.8
e) 0.941 **f)** 0.874
g) 18.69 **h)** 4.065
i) 2.9 **j)** 17.6
k) 3.9 **l)** 9.9
m) 24.9 **n)** 0.1
o) 7.93 **p)** 73.065
q) 0.008 **r)** 2.04
s) 14.83 **t)** 4.91
6 **a)** 1.567 **b)** 1.383
c) 0.971 **d)** 2.733
e) 88.333 **f)** 41.429
g) 3.282 **h)** 6.317
i) 72.889
7 **a)** **i)** 46.1448 **ii)** 46.145
iii) 46.14 **iv)** 46.1
b) **i)** 59.6970 **ii)** 59.697
iii) 59.70 **iv)** 59.7
c) **i)** 569.4337 **ii)** 569.434
iii) 569.43 **iv)** 569.4
d) **i)** 17.0588 **ii)** 17.059
iii) 17.06 **iv)** 17.1
e) **i)** 0.6627 **ii)** 0.663
iii) 0.66 **iv)** 0.7
f) **i)** 3.4200 **ii)** 3.420
iii) 3.42 **iv)** 3.4
8 **a)** $12.16 **b)** $2.37
c) $1.33 **d)** $15.35

Exercise 3

1 a) 20   b) 500
      c) 0.3   d) 0.02
      e) 20   f) 30
2 a) 2730   b) 3060
      c) 0.0124   d) 0.0316
      e) 42 600   f) 86 300
      g) 240 000   h) 1 100 000
      i) 0.007 01   j) 0.000 497
3 a) i) 1.82   ii) 1.8
      b) i) 0.07   ii) 0.071
      c) i) 8.06   ii) 8.1
      d) i) 4567.12   ii) 4600
4 a) 460 000   b) 450 000
      c) 7 980 000   d) 8 000 000
      e) 1300   f) 20 000
      g) 0.000 57   h) 0.094
      i) 0.0937   j) 0.093 75
      k) 0.010   l) 0.030
5 472 m^2 (correct to 3 s.f.)
6 a) i) 82 656   ii) 82 660
        iii) 82 700   iv) 83 000
      b) i) 82.656   ii) 82.66
        iii) 82.7   iv) 83
      c) i) 1000.96   ii) 1001
        iii) 1000   iv) 1000
      d) i) 0.007 281   ii) 0.007 281
        iii) 0.007 28   iv) 0.0073
      e) i) 0.001 898 9   ii) 0.001 899
        iii) 0.001 90   iv) 0.0019
      f) i) 3.42   ii) 3.420
        iii) 3.42   iv) 3.4

Exercise 4

1 4 trips
2 5 tables
3 10 times
4 5 buses
5 17 packs
6 24 parking spaces
7 30 bags
8 15 letters
9 5 oranges
10 7 packs
11 3 packs

Exercise 5

1 a) i) 1200   ii) 1312
      b) i) 700   ii) 792
      c) i) 1800   ii) 1972
      d) i) 3500   ii) 3240
      e) i) 2400   ii) 2652
      f) i) 4000   ii) 3723
      g) i) 18 000   ii) 16 296
      h) i) 6000   ii) 7176
2 a) i) 30   ii) 33
      b) i) 30   ii) 29
      c) i) 15   ii) 16
      d) i) 20   ii) 24
3 a) i) 8   ii) 7.56
      b) i) 27   ii) 27.59
      c) i) 200   ii) 202.02
      d) i) 300   ii) 299.86
4 a) i) 2   ii) 2.2
      b) i) 5   ii) 4.8
      c) i) 10   ii) 9.5
      d) i) 40   ii) 39.9
5 a) $5800   b) $6112
6 a) 1500 people   b) 1500 more people
7 a) i) 6.4   ii) 6.418 75
      b) i) 20   ii) 18.85
      c) i) 20   ii) 20.456 31
      d) i) 10   ii) 10.127 93

Unit 8 Measures and measurement

Exercise 1

1 a) minutes
   b) weeks or months
   c) hours
   d) seconds
   e) minutes or seconds
   f) years
   g) minutes
   h) seconds
   i) weeks or months
   j) hours

2 a) 30 minutes
   b) 45 minutes
   c) 140 minutes
   d) 255 minutes
   e) 350 minutes
   f) 460 minutes
   g) 915 minutes
   h) 1210 minutes
   i) 1680 minutes

3 a) 12 hours   b) 18 hours
   c) 56 hours   d) 102 hours
   e) 140 hours   f) 184 hours
   g) 240 hours   h) 276 hours
   i) 390 hours

4 a) 120 hours
   b) 180 minutes
   c) 360 minutes
   d) 4 minutes
   e) 4 days
   f) 6 hours
   g) $4\frac{1}{6}$ hours
   h) 1500 seconds
   i) $4\frac{1}{6}$ days
   j) $3\frac{2}{3}$ hours
   k) 84 hours
   l) 165 minutes

5 a) 6 hours 31 minutes
   b) 11 hours 49 minutes
   c) 3 hours 56 minutes
   d) 7 hours 30 minutes
   e) 11 hours 4 minutes
   f) 11 hours 22 minutes
   g) 9 hours 27 minutes
   h) 5 hours 5 minutes
   i) 4 hours 59 minutes

6 a) 08 50
   b) 11 22
   c) 00 42
   d) 01 05
   e) 02 53
   f) 16 15
   g) 19 38
   h) 15 12
   i) 21 43
   j) 23 50

7 a) 2.30 a.m.
   b) 7.40 a.m.
   c) 12.15 a.m.
   d) 11.12 a.m.
   e) 12.00 noon
   f) 7.00 p.m.
   g) 1.42 p.m.
   h) 8.20 p.m.
   i) 10.32 p.m.
   j) 11.10 p.m.

8 a) 10 hours
   b) 20 hours
   c) 11 hours
   d) 9 hours
   e) 17 hours 5 minutes
   f) 6 hours
   g) 15 hours
   h) 11 hours
   i) 11 hours

9 a) 6 hours
   b) 16 hours
   c) 18 hours
   d) 5 hours 45 minutes
   e) 22 hours 16 minutes
   f) 8 hours
   g) 19 hours
   h) 9 hours
   i) 20 hours 18 minutes

10 a) 18 35, 19 20, 20 00, 20 50
   b) 40 minutes
   c) 45 minutes

11 a) 13 15, 16 05
   b) 2 hours 50 minutes

12 a) 11 10, 15 25
   b) 4 hours 15 minutes

13 a) 01 30
   b) 1.30 a.m.

14 a) 14 41
   b) 2.41 p.m.

15 a) 8.15 a.m. or 18 15
   b) 5.30 p.m. or 17 30

Exercise 2

1. a) m or cm   b) mm
   c) cm or mm   d) km
   e) mm   f) cm
   g) km   h) km or m
2. a) × 10   b) ÷ 100
   c) × 1000   d) ÷ 1000
   e) × 100 000   f) ÷ 1000
   g) ÷ 100 000   h) × 100
3. b) 6, 6000   c) 850, 8.5
   d) 4.5, 45   e) 1.34, 1340
   f) 72.6, 0.0726   g) 12.6, 1260
   h) 4820, 4.82
4. b) 1000, 45 000   c) 1000, 0.25
   d) 10, 7.4   e) 1000, 2200
   f) 10, 380   g) 10, 45
   h) 1000, 0.305
5. a) 3000 m   b) 5600 m
   c) 6340 m   d) 7500 m
6. a) 1100 cm   b) 63 cm
   c) 359 cm   d) 1350 cm
7. a) 350 mm   b) 5.2 mm
   c) 58.3 mm   d) 55 mm
8. a) 50 000 mm   b) 70 mm
   c) 4321 mm   d) 3750 mm
9. a) 300 cm   b) 4000 m
   c) 2000 mm   d) 100 mm
   e) 4900 m   f) 5130 mm
   g) 6820 cm   h) 52.4 m
   i) 3710 cm   j) 3100 m
   k) 65 mm   l) 2700 mm
10. a) 60 000 mm   b) 5 cm
    c) 5.5 m   d) 0.682 km
    e) 0.004 82 km   f) 0.926 m
    g) 43 000 mm   h) 6 000 000 cm
    i) 141 000 mm

Exercise 3

1. a) g or kg   b) kg
   c) tonne   d) g
   e) g or kg   f) tonne
   g) mg   h) mg
2. a) × 1000   b) ÷ 1000
   c) × 1 000 000   d) ÷ 1 000 000
   e) × 1 000 000   f) ÷ 1000
   g) ÷ 1 000 000   h) × 1000
3. a) 205 g   b) 2300 g
   c) 487.5 g   d) 9027 g
4. a) 0.006 kg   b) 0.089 kg
   c) 0.2687 kg   d) 0.016 32 kg

5. a) 3540 kg   b) 800 kg
   c) 12 017 kg   d) 23 704 kg
6. a) 0.008 t   b) 0.56 t
   c) 9.101 t   d) 0.6789 t
7. a) 2750 mg   b) 500 mg
   c) 730 mg   d) 13 580 mg
8. a) 3000 g   b) 5600 g
   c) 6340 g   d) 7500 g
9. a) 0.64 g   b) 0.06 g
   c) 0.007 g   d) 9 g
10. a) 6200 g   b) 4.56 t
    c) 5500 g   d) 470 000 kg
    e) 0.609 t   f) 2250 kg
    g) 5500 kg   h) 0.068 kg
    i) 5.28 g   j) 9060 mg
    k) 0.000 963 t   l) 740 g
11. 4.843 kg
12. 2.34 g
13. 4.196 t
14. 400 bags

Exercise 4

1. a) litre   b) ml
   c) litre   d) ml
   e) ml   f) ml or litre
   g) ml   h) litre
2. a) 75 litre   b) 69 000 ml
   c) 4530 ml   d) 13 870 ml
   e) 5.35 litre   f) 4.58 litre
   g) 5500 ml   h) 7250 ml
   i) 0.028 litre
3. a) 109 000 ml   b) 7350 ml
   c) 14 280 ml   d) 54.5 litre
   e) 96.5 litre   f) 33 673 ml
   g) 81.55 litre   h) 59.05 litre
4. 525 ml
5. 274 ml
6. 775 ml left

Exercise 5

1. d) 30 g
2. c) 30 cm
3. e) 200 ml
4. a) 3.5 cm or 35 mm
   b) 100 m
   c) 10 g
   d) 1 t
5. about 7.5 m
6. about 17 m

Unit 9 An introduction to algebra

Exercise 1

1 a) v) $3x$
    b) i) $x + 3$
  c) vi) $3 - x$
    d) iii) $x - 3$
  e) vii) $\dfrac{x}{3}$
    f) iv) $3x + 8$

  g) ii) $3x - 8$

2 a) iv) $4x - 7$
    b) i) $7 - 4x$
  c) ii) $2x - 9$
    d) vi) $9 - 2x$
  e) vii) $\dfrac{x}{2} - 9$
    f) iii) $7x + 4$

  g) v) $7x + 4x$

3 a) ii) $x + 9$
    b) vi) $x - 15$
  c) i) $x + 15$
    d) iv) $2x - 9$
  e) v) $2x + 9$
    f) iii) $4x - 9$

  g) vii) $\dfrac{3}{4}x - 9$

4 a) $2c$
    b) $2d$
  c) $2e$
    d) $f - 3$
  e) $\dfrac{3}{y}$
    f) $hk + 5$
  g) $6 - mn$
    h) $\dfrac{p + q}{r}$
  i) $\dfrac{st}{u}$
    j) $y - \dfrac{x}{4}$
  k) $(b - a)c$
    l) $xy + hk$
  m) $a + 2b$
    n) $2(a + b)$
  o) $30 - 3c$
    p) $3(30 - c)$
  q) $50 - 10p$
    r) $50(p + 10)$
  s) $100 + \dfrac{x}{y}$
    t) $\dfrac{x}{y + 100}$
  u) $\dfrac{a}{2} + 25b$
    v) $4c - \dfrac{d}{5}$
  w) $\dfrac{m + 2n}{2}$
    x) $60 - \dfrac{7x}{3}$

Exercise 2

1 a) 15
    b) -11
  c) 10
    d) -5
  e) 6
    f) 11
  g) 10
    h) 18
  i) 6
    j) -16
  k) -5
    l) 5
  m) 5
    n) 9
  o) 9
    p) 50
  q) -5
    r) $\dfrac{5}{9}$
  s) 12
    t) $-2\dfrac{9}{10}$

2 a) 120
    b) 33
  c) 12
    d) 26
  e) 24
    f) 24

Exercise 3

1 a) constant
    b) variable
  c) variable
    d) variable
  e) variable
    f) constant

2 a) $+7$
    b) -5
  c) $+1$
    d) -4

3 a) $+1$
  b) $+4$
  c) no constant term
  d) $+5$

4 a) 2
    b) 1
  c) 3
    d) 3
  e) 1
    f) 4
  g) 3
    h) 3
  i) 1
    j) 2

5 a) $5a$ and $-2a$
  b) m^2 and $-3m^2$
  c) $-3hk$ and kh
  d) ab and $7ba$
  e) no like terms
  f) $-2ef$ and $6fe$
  g) $2yb^2$ and $-5b^2y$
  h) no like terms
  i) $17e$ and $-4e$, 16 and -3
  j) $4mn$ and $-nm$, $2n$ and $3n$
  k) -3 and 5
  l) $3d^2$ and d^2, $-2g$ and $-g$

Exercise 4

1 a) $3c$ b) $5x$
   c) $2t$ d) d
   e) $3n$ f) $5y$
   g) $10g$ h) $7z$
   i) $3j$ j) $4c$
   k) $7x$ l) w
   m) 0 n) $-5y$
   o) $-5x$ p) $-14a$
   q) $6b$ r) $-4m$

2 a) $8x + y$ b) $w + 2v$
   c) $2a - 2b$ d) $5x + 3y$
   e) $3 + 7u$ f) $p + 4q$
   g) $3d - 7c$ h) $2y + 1$
   i) $a + b$ j) $4m + n$
   k) $9c - d$ l) $x + y$
   m) $6p$ n) $5 - 5k$
   o) $a + 3$ p) $-s - t - 5$

3 a) $8a + 3b$ b) $3p + 3q$
   c) $3m + 2n$ d) $x - 2y$
   e) $2x + 3y$ f) $d + 3$
   g) $3b - 2a$ h) 7
   i) $a + 2b$ j) $-2f$
   k) $v - 4w$ l) $-5t - 2$
   m) $4q - 4p$ n) $1 - 7k$
   o) $c - d + 11$ p) $3n - 2m - 6$

4 a) $2xy$
   b) $2pq$
   c) $3ab$
   d) $2x^2$
   e) $9y^2$
   f) $4a^2$
   g) $15ev - 2e$
   h) $8gh + 2g + 4h$
   i) $3mn + 2n + 3n^2$
   j) $12jp + 5j - 14p$
   k) $2rk$
   l) cannot be simplified

5 a) $\frac{1}{6}b$ b) $1\frac{4}{5}d$
   c) $\frac{11}{12}f$ d) $1\frac{1}{2}b - k$
   e) $\frac{1}{8}x - \frac{1}{7}y$ f) $\frac{1}{18}j^2 - \frac{1}{3}p$
   g) $1\frac{1}{6}uv$ h) $\frac{1}{10}mn + m$

6 a) i) $a + 2b$ ii) 13
   b) i) $6a + 4b$ ii) 54
   c) i) $2a + 2b$ ii) 20
   d) i) $4a - 7b$ ii) 7
   e) i) $5a - 8b$ ii) 11
   f) i) $9ab - 3b$ ii) 180

Exercise 5

1 a) $9a + 6b$
   b) $3x + y + z$
   c) $2b + 10c + 10$
   d) $15x + y - 4z$
   e) $3a + 3b + 3c - 7$
   f) $6ab + 3cd + 10xy$
   g) $2x^2y + 5xy^2 + 2y^3$
   h) $-\frac{1}{2}x^2 + 3\frac{1}{2}xy + 3y^2$
   i) $7\frac{5}{6} - 2x^2 + 4ab$

2 a) $-xy^2$
   b) $10x^2y - 3xy^2$
   c) $4a + 2b - 3d$
   d) $3a + 7b$
   e) $2x^3 - x^2 + 4x + 7$
   f) $a^3 - 3a^2 - 2a - 2$
   g) $2abc + 6bcd + 3cda$
   h) $3a^2 - 4ab + b^2$
   i) $-8x^2 + 10x - 12$
   j) $6a + 7b + 14c$
   k) $3m^2 - m - 1$
   l) $3y - 6$
   m) $10ab - 8bc + 16cd$

Exercise 6

1 a) $3a$ b) $7b$ c) $8c$
   d) $9d$ e) $4e$ f) $8f$
   g) $6p$ h) $15q$ i) r^2
   j) g^2 k) $2g^2$ l) $12g^2$
   m) $4t^2$ n) $15u^2$ o) $9d^2$

2 a) $-3y$ b) $-5y$ c) $2y$
   d) $-6y$ e) $-t^2$ f) $-2t^2$
   g) $-10t^2$ h) $10t^2$ i) $-10m^3$

3 a) $5a$ b) $4b$
   c) 12 d) 20
   e) $2y$ f) 2
   g) 18 h) $3p$
   i) 9 j) 6
   k) 4 l) 5
   m) 4 n) 9
   o) $\dfrac{d}{3}$

4 a) $-2y$ b) $-3y$
   c) -5 d) m
   e) -3 f) -2
   g) -3 h) $\frac{1}{2}$
   i) $-4t^2$

5 a) ab

   b) xy

   c) $3y^2$

   d) $2pq$

   e) $2a^2$

   f) $5xy$

   g) $6ab$

   h) $12gh$

   i) $6d^2$

   j) $3g^2$

   k) $5ab$

   l) $6gh$

   m) abc

   n) m^3

   o) $2d^3$

   p) $6x^3$

   q) $3g^3$

   r) $10m^2n$

   s) $3ab^2c$

   t) $18pqr$

   u) $21st^2u$

6 a) y^3

   b) t^5

   c) $-a^6$

   d) g^{10}

   e) $-a^4$

   f) $-m^6$

   g) $2y^3$

   h) $6d^5$

   i) $8x^5$

   j) $-25y^6$

   k) $-24r^6$

   l) m^3n^2

   m) a^4b^2

   n) $6r^3s^4$

   o) $10x^5y^3$

7 a) y^2

   b) a

   c) -1

   d) t^4

   e) $\dfrac{1}{g}$

   f) $\dfrac{1}{b^2}$

   g) $6b^2$

   h) $5m$

   i) $4x^6$

   j) $-4t$

   k) $\dfrac{3}{b}$

   l) y

   m) $\dfrac{m^2}{n}$

   n) $\dfrac{2p^2}{3q}$

   o) $3rs^2$

8 a) t

   b) $\dfrac{1}{g}$

   c) m^2

   d) y

   e) y^2

   f) $\dfrac{1}{m}$

   g) $2t^2$

   h) $\dfrac{-3}{b}$

   i) $-6ab^2$

Exercise 7

1 a) $b^2 + 7b$

   b) $d^2 - 4d$

   c) $3f^2 + 4f$

   d) $12h^2 - 15h$

   e) $-2z^2 - 3z$

   f) $-4y^2 - y$

   g) $-12k^2 + 20ks$

   h) $-2ab + 6ac$

   i) $4n^2 + 3n$

   j) $5x + 5y - 20$

   k) $6d^2 + 8de - d^2e$

   l) $-6pm - 18p^2$

2 a) $2x + 5$

   b) $3a + 11$

   c) $6w - 17$

   d) $10 + 2p$

   e) $3q$

   f) $7 - 3t$

   g) $5z + 8$

   h) $8t + 15$

   i) $2c - 6$

   j) $5a - 9$

   k) $3y - 10$

   l) $2x + 6$

   m) $8a + 23$

   n) $10x - 12$

   o) $2p - 11$

   p) $5a + 2b$

   q) $3x + y$

   r) $5x - x^2$

   s) $a^2 - 2a$

   t) $2y$

   u) $2d + 6$

   v) $2x^2$

   w) $7t^2 - 6t$

   x) $8m - 2m^2$

3 a) $7x + 34$

   b) $11t - 23$

   c) $14r + 31$

   d) $34y - 33$

   e) $a + 4$

   f) $a + 17$

   g) $2x + 8$

   h) $9t + 1$

   i) $2m^2 + 7m$

   j) $12n^2 + 45n$

   k) $-5p^2 - 36p$

   l) $-11y^2 - 19y$

   m) $-13a^2 - 22a$

   n) $-7a^2 + 2a$

   o) $2z^2 + z$

   p) $9a + 5$

   q) $26t + 30$

   r) $z + 17$

   s) $-8q - 44$

   t) $-19x - 33$

   u) $16e^2 - 4e - 8$

   v) $8 + 20d - 2d^2$

   w) $7m^2 - 5m$

   x) $-11a^2 + 8a$

Unit 10 An introduction to geometry

Exercise 1

1 a) $\overline{AB} = 2.3\,$cm

  b) $\overline{AC} = 7.1\,$cm

  c) $\overline{BC} = 4.8\,$cm

  d) $\overline{CE} = 6.9\,$cm

  e) $\overline{DE} = 2.8\,$cm

  f) $\overline{DF} = 3.9\,$cm

2 a) $\overline{PQ} = 4.9\,$cm

  b) $\overline{QR} = 2.2\,$cm

  c) $\overline{RS} = 3.1\,$cm

  d) $\overline{ST} = 4.3\,$cm

  e) $\overline{TP} = 3.1\,$cm

3 $\overline{AB}, \overline{BC}, \overline{CD}, \overline{AC}, \overline{AD}, \overline{BD}$

4 190 line segments

Exercise 2

1 a) Two of $\angle CBA, \angle ABC, \angle B, C\hat{B}A, A\hat{B}C, \hat{B}$

  b) Two of $\angle PQR, \angle RQP, \angle Q, P\hat{Q}R, R\hat{Q}P, \hat{Q}$

  c) Two of $\angle DEF, \angle FED, \angle E, D\hat{E}F, F\hat{E}D, \hat{E}$

  d) Two of $\angle XYZ, \angle ZYX, \angle Y, X\hat{Y}Z, Z\hat{Y}X, \hat{Y}$

2 a) acute angle

  b) right angle

  c) obtuse angle

  d) acute angle

  e) obtuse angle

  f) obtuse angle

  g) reflex angle

  h) reflex angle

Exercise 3

1 a) $\angle DOC = 29°$

  b) $\hat{O} = 45°$

  c) $A\hat{B}C = 18°$

  d) $\angle XYZ = 96°$

  e) $\angle PQR = 156°$

  f) $\angle TNK = 241°$

  g) $F\hat{E}R = 136°$

  h) $\angle U = 325°$

2 Check pupils' diagrams.

Exercise 4

1 a) $80°$ b) $30°$

  c) $25°$ d) $78°$

  e) $16°$ f) $7°$

  g) $85°$ h) $52°$

2 a) $168°$ b) $154°$

  c) $62°$ d) $76°$

  e) $44°$ f) $27°$

  g) $1°$ h) $119°$

3 a) supplementary

  b) supplementary

  c) complementary

  d) complementary

  e) supplementary

  f) supplementary

  g) supplementary

  h) supplementary

  i) complementary

  j) complementary

4 a) $a = 31°$

  b) $b = 146°$

  c) $c = 38°$

  d) $d = 20°$

  e) $e = 126°$

  f) $f = 198°$

  g) $g = 135°, h = 45°$

  h) $i = 126°$

  i) $j = 119°, k = 61°, l = 29°$

  j) $m = 105°$

  k) $n = 49°, p = 41°$

  l) $q = 97°, r = 26°, s = 57°$

5 a) $x = 45°$ b) $x = 30°$

  c) $x = 60°$ d) $x = 36°$

  e) $x = 28°$ f) $x = 59°$

  g) $x = 20°$ h) $x = 23°$

Exercise 5

Check pupils' diagrams.

Unit 11 An introduction to coordinate geometry

Exercise 1

1 $A(1, 2)$
$B(4, 1)$
$C(-2, 4)$
$D(-1, 1)$
$E(-4, -2)$
$F(-2, -5)$
$G(2, -1)$
$H(4, -4)$
$I(5, 0)$
$J(-3, 0)$
$K(0, 4)$
$L(0, -2)$

2 $A\left(1\frac{1}{2}, \frac{1}{2}\right)$

$B\left(3, 4\frac{1}{2}\right)$

$C\left(0, 1\frac{1}{2}\right)$

$D\left(-1\frac{1}{2}, 3\right)$

$E\left(-3\frac{1}{2}, 5\right)$

$F\left(-4\frac{1}{2}, 0\right)$

$G\left(-3\frac{1}{2}, -1\frac{1}{2}\right)$

$H\left(-2\frac{1}{2}, -2\frac{1}{2}\right)$

$I\left(0, -4\frac{1}{2}\right)$

$J\left(2, -3\frac{1}{2}\right)$

$K\left(5, -2\frac{1}{2}\right)$

$L\left(4\frac{1}{2}, 0\right)$

3 Check pupils' graphs.
4 Check pupils' graphs.

5

Point	x-coordinate (+ or −)	y-coordinate (+ or −)	Quadrant
$A(3, 2)$	+	+	1st
$B(-1, 4)$	−	+	2nd
$C(2, -3)$	+	−	4th
$D(-4, -1)$	−	−	3rd
$E(2, -5)$	+	−	4th
$F(-3, 1)$	−	+	2nd
$G(5, -2)$	+	−	4th
$H(-6, -3)$	−	−	3rd
$I(-2, 4)$	−	+	2nd
$J(1, 5)$	+	+	1st
$K(4, -1)$	+	−	4th

6 **a), b)** Check pupils' graphs.
star
7 **a), b)** Check pupils' graphs.
dog
8 **a), b)** Check pupils' graphs.
straight line
9 **a), b)** Check pupils' graphs.
parabola

Answers to the Workbook

Unit 1 Integers

1 a) 515
    b) 7089
    c) 33 000
    d) 406 000
    e) 2 100 000
    f) 3 009 054
    g) 67 000 000 043
    h) 40 801

2 a) eleven
    b) two hundred and thirteen
    c) three thousand, eight hundred and sixty-seven
    d) forty-three thousand, two hundred and ninety-one
    e) six hundred and forty thousand, five hundred and fifty-two
    f) seven million, eight hundred and forty-nine thousand, three hundred and sixty
    g) four hundred and four thousand, nine hundred and six
    h) fifteen million, and twenty
    i) three hundred and one million, two hundred thousand, and five
    j) twelve thousand, and seventeen

3 a) 56
    b) 44
    c) 29
    d) 266
    e) 152
    f) 68
    g) 120
    h) 300
    i) 150
    j) 130
    k) 81 900
    l) 38 850
    m) 730 300
    n) 288 200
    o) 4900
    p) 111 000
    q) 111 100
    r) 6600
    s) 5600
    t) 456
    u) 200

4 a) 15
    b) 26
    c) 50
    d) 108
    e) 8
    f) 31
    g) 23
    h) 34
    i) 27
    j) 31
    k) 47
    l) 18
    m) 6
    n) 11
    o) 116
    p) 98
    q) 189
    r) 136
    s) 36
    t) 37
    u) 139
    v) 120
    w) 21
    x) 9
    y) 9
    z) 12

5 a) 16
    b) 25
    c) 4
    d) 17
    e) 10
    f) 315
    g) 270
    h) 63
    i) 114
    j) 270
    k) 108
    l) 87
    m) 210
    n) 37
    o) 80
    p) 2
    q) 8
    r) 33
    s) 4
    t) 189
    u) 655
    v) 4
    w) 36
    x) 10
    y) 135
    z) 539

6 a) 0
    b) −50
    c) −65
    d) −10
    e) −20
    f) 5
    g) 1
    h) −1
    i) 80
    j) 20
    k) −10
    l) 20
    m) −5
    n) −20
    o) 10
    p) −20
    q) 0
    r) 100
    s) −16
    t) 2
    u) 19

7 a) −420
    b) 180
    c) 900
    d) 120
    e) −320
    f) −280
    g) −630
    h) −720
    i) −1200
    j) 120
    k) 360
    l) −1280
    m) −400
    n) −156
    o) 9000

8 a) 25
    b) 3
    c) −125
    d) −8
    e) −7
    f) −7
    g) −5
    h) −3
    i) 9
    j) 4
    k) 3
    l) −4
    m) −3
    n) −5
    o) −6

9 a) −3
    b) 8
    c) −1
    d) −2
    e) −4
    f) 2
    g) −3
    h) 1
    i) 2
    j) −2
    k) −280
    l) −500
    m) 268
    n) 9
    o) 294
    p) 240

10 1332 m

11 a) 106 °C
    b) 29 °C

12 $758

13 €6

14 132 children

Unit 2 Factors and multiples

1 a) $3 \times 5 \times 11^2$
b) $2^3 \times 5 \times 7 \times 13$
c) $2 \times 3 \times 5 \times 7 \times 11$
d) $2^3 \times 3 \times 11$
e) $3^3 \times 7$
f) $2^3 \times 5^2 \times 19 \times 31$
g) $2^7 \times 3^3 \times 17$
h) $2^4 \times 3^2 \times 5^2 \times 17$
i) $2^3 \times 7 \times 11 \times 13$
j) $2 \times 3 \times 7^2 \times 11$
k) $2^2 \times 3^2 \times 7 \times 13^2$
l) $5 \times 7^2 \times 11^2$
m) $2^2 \times 3^2 \times 11 \times 13$
n) $5^2 \times 7 \times 11$
o) $2 \times 3 \times 7 \times 11 \times 13$
p) $2^3 \times 3 \times 7^3 \times 17$
q) $3^2 \times 11^2 \times 13 \times 31$
r) $3^3 \times 7 \times 13 \times 23$
s) $3^2 \times 5^3 \times 7^2 \times 17$
t) $2^7 \times 3 \times 7^2 \times 13$
u) $2^6 \times 3^2 \times 11 \times 17$

2 a) 6 b) 6
c) 14 d) 15
e) 8 f) 16
g) 5 h) 7
i) 8 j) 12
k) 28 l) 9
m) 3 n) 18
o) 33 p) 4
q) 9 r) 14
s) 78 t) 72
u) 56 v) 22

3 a) 9 b) 12
c) 21 d) 16
e) 6 f) 14
g) 15 h) 21
i) 15 j) 12
k) 504 l) 63
m) 132 n) 735
o) 78 p) 528
q) 150 r) 88
s) 252

4 a) 18 b) 30
c) 21 d) 24
e) 36 f) 75
g) 72 h) 150
i) 1755 j) 162
k) 300 l) 1080
m) 144 n) 1575
o) 4410 p) 800
q) 250 r) 525
s) 144 t) 120
u) 5544 v) 2448
w) 1215 x) 1305
y) 8820

5 a) 90 b) 48
c) 72 d) 126
e) 5236 f) 61 425
g) 72 h) 72
i) 13 104 j) 46 800
k) 13 500 l) 54 054
m) 8316 n) 1260
o) 3276 p) 20 944
q) 6804 r) 1890
s) 25 872 t) 9450
u) 32 760

6 a) HCF = 13, LCM = 78
b) HCF = 7, LCM = 84
c) HCF = 6, LCM = 126
d) HCF = 112, LCM = 672
e) HCF = 15, LCM = 450
f) HCF = 70, LCM = 420
g) HCF = 252, LCM = 7056
h) HCF = 56, LCM = 4312
i) HCF = 45, LCM = 5040
j) HCF = 21, LCM = 756
k) HCF = 35, LCM = 12 600
l) HCF = 66, LCM = 11 880
m) HCF = 63, LCM = 2268
n) HCF = 28, LCM = 1120
o) HCF = 42, LCM = 7560
p) HCF = 18, LCM = 1296

7 10 p.m. or 22 00

Unit 3 Fractions

1 a) $\frac{7}{18}, \frac{11}{27}, \frac{5}{12}$ b) $\frac{37}{45}, \frac{5}{6}, \frac{13}{15}$

   c) $\frac{13}{20}, \frac{11}{15}, \frac{3}{4}$ d) $\frac{13}{20}, \frac{2}{3}, \frac{7}{10}$

   e) $\frac{13}{16}, \frac{5}{6}, \frac{7}{8}$ f) $\frac{11}{20}, \frac{9}{16}, \frac{23}{40}, \frac{3}{5}$

2 a) $\frac{4}{5}, \frac{3}{4}, \frac{2}{3}$ b) $\frac{7}{9}, \frac{13}{18}, \frac{19}{27}$

   c) $\frac{14}{25}, \frac{53}{100}, \frac{26}{50}$ d) $\frac{17}{24}, \frac{11}{16}, \frac{5}{8}$

   e) $\frac{7}{9}, \frac{3}{4}, \frac{13}{18}$ f) $\frac{13}{15}, \frac{5}{6}, \frac{7}{9}, \frac{23}{30}$

3 a) $1\frac{1}{2}$ b) $\frac{2}{3}$

   c) $\frac{1}{4}$ d) $\frac{2}{5}$

   e) $\frac{13}{24}$ f) $1\frac{1}{3}$

   g) $\frac{1}{6}$ h) $\frac{1}{24}$

   i) $13\frac{7}{12}$ j) $2\frac{13}{36}$

4 a) $3\frac{11}{12}$ b) $1\frac{3}{8}$

   c) $\frac{13}{24}$ d) 1

   e) $\frac{7}{16}$ f) $3\frac{9}{14}$

   g) $3\frac{28}{45}$ h) $2\frac{19}{24}$

5 a) $1\frac{1}{2}$ b) $\frac{1}{6}$

   c) $1\frac{1}{2}$ d) 4

   e) 5 f) 4

   g) $\frac{4}{7}$ h) $15\frac{3}{4}$

   i) 1 j) $1\frac{2}{3}$

6 a) $-3\frac{1}{30}$ b) $-\frac{2}{21}$

   c) $\frac{1}{4}$ d) $-81\frac{1}{2}$

   e) 10 f) -36

   g) $-1\frac{1}{44}$ h) -4

   i) $1\frac{1}{9}$ j) $-\frac{3}{11}$

   k) $\frac{2}{13}$ l) $4\frac{1}{2}$

7 a) $3\frac{5}{12}$ b) $3\frac{2}{3}$

   c) $\frac{11}{20}$ d) $\frac{9}{10}$

   e) $\frac{1}{10}$ f) $1\frac{1}{7}$

   g) $1\frac{1}{3}$ h) $1\frac{6}{7}$

   i) $\frac{1}{2}$ j) 6

   k) $1\frac{3}{16}$ l) -3

   m) $-\frac{3}{5}$ n) 2

   o) $-1\frac{1}{12}$ p) $-\frac{1}{11}$

8 a) $1\frac{1}{4}$ b) $2\frac{2}{3}$

   c) $\frac{5}{6}$ d) $8\frac{1}{5}$

   e) $1\frac{4}{25}$ f) $3\frac{1}{3}$

   g) $\frac{5}{6}$ h) $\frac{4}{7}$

   i) $\frac{2}{15}$ j) $\frac{5}{26}$

   k) $\frac{8}{33}$ l) $\frac{3}{8}$

   m) 4 n) $\frac{40}{47}$

   o) $23\frac{1}{3}$

9 a) $\frac{1}{4}$ b) €280 000

10 $24

11 £2160

12 a) $\frac{2}{9}$ b) $\frac{1}{6}$

13 28 sweets

14 17 boys

Unit 4 Decimals

1 a) $(4 \times 10) + (6 \times 1) + \left(6 \times \frac{1}{100}\right)$

b) $(1 \times 10) + \left(9 \times \frac{1}{100}\right) + \left(6 \times \frac{1}{1000}\right)$

c) $\left(8 \times \frac{1}{1000}\right) + \left(1 \times \frac{1}{10\,000}\right)$

$+ \left(7 \times \frac{1}{100\,000}\right) + \left(5 \times \frac{1}{1\,000\,000}\right)$

d) $(1 \times 100) + (3 \times 10)$

$+ (8 \times 1) + \left(8 \times \frac{1}{100}\right)$

e) $(6 \times 1000) + (5 \times 100) + (4 \times 10)$

$+ (3 \times 1) + \left(2 \times \frac{1}{10}\right) + \left(1 \times \frac{1}{1000}\right)$

f) $(9 \times 1) + \left(5 \times \frac{1}{10}\right) + \left(7 \times \frac{1}{100}\right)$

$+ \left(3 \times \frac{1}{1000}\right) + \left(6 \times \frac{1}{10\,000}\right)$

2 a) 0.3   b) 0.07
c) 0.005   d) 0.48
e) 0.013   f) 8.2
g) 7.04   h) 13.009
i) 20.08   j) 78.52
k) 400.079   l) 700.405
m) 90.607   n) 815.9001

3 a) 8.062   b) 2.323
c) 8.33   d) 38.45
e) 27.45   f) 5.54
g) 1.48   h) 8.659
i) 1.326   j) 0.25
k) 12.444   l) 2.9

4 a) 0.244 02   b) 0.13
c) 15.539   d) 5.8
e) 2.983   f) 15.140 68
g) 4.79   h) 12.75
i) 3.32   j) 2440.2
k) 290   l) 0.009
m) 250   n) 42.9866
o) 2.54   p) 2
q) 8.875   r) 0.2
s) 46.8   t) 2.484

5 a) 20.07   b) 7.12
c) 5   d) 51.95
e) 7.08   f) 39.914
g) 1.26   h) 0.01
i) 83.64   j) 26.31
k) 402   l) 24
m) 71.63   n) 1.6
o) 34   p) 12.5
q) 200   r) 10.075
s) 6.3   t) 16

6 a) 0.47   b) 0.083
c) 0.0132   d) 1.15
e) 3.175   f) 2.6875
g) 53.36   h) 0.512
i) 14.531 25   j) 1.6875
k) 0.215   l) 2.024
m) 2.62   n) 0.875
o) 0.548

7 a) $\frac{3}{500}$ b) $\frac{16}{125}$
c) $\frac{3}{40}$ d) $\frac{21}{200}$
e) $\frac{4}{625}$ f) $\frac{27}{50}$
g) $\frac{7}{20}$ h) $\frac{43}{50}$
i) $23\frac{7}{200}$ j) $7\frac{187}{200}$
k) $8\frac{12}{125}$ l) $47\frac{12}{25}$
m) $9\frac{143}{200}$ n) $13\frac{9}{25}$
o) $76\frac{5}{8}$

8 a) $0.29\overset{\bullet}{5}\overset{\bullet}{4}$ b) $0.\overset{\bullet}{5}\overset{\bullet}{9}$
c) $0.6\overset{\bullet}{7}$ d) $2.\overset{\bullet}{3}$
e) $1.6\overset{\bullet}{1}$ f) $0.91\overset{\bullet}{6}$
g) $0.2\overset{\bullet}{5}\overset{\bullet}{7}$ h) $0.\overset{\bullet}{5}$
i) $0.486\overset{\bullet}{1}$ j) $0.\overset{\bullet}{5}71\,42\overset{\bullet}{8}$
k) $0.2\overset{\bullet}{2}\overset{\bullet}{7}$ l) $0.\overset{\bullet}{8}\overset{\bullet}{7}$
m) $0.\overset{\bullet}{4}\overset{\bullet}{5}$ n) $1.0\overset{\bullet}{4}$
o) $0.763\overset{\bullet}{8}$ p) $0.395\,8\overset{\bullet}{3}$
q) $0.8\overset{\bullet}{4}0\overset{\bullet}{9}$ r) $0.\overset{\bullet}{1}0\overset{\bullet}{0}$
s) $0.\overset{\bullet}{3}9\overset{\bullet}{9}$ t) $0.00\overset{\bullet}{8}1\overset{\bullet}{3}$

9 15 packets
10 $35.52
11 Shop A
12 $16.10
13 a) $13.44   b) $6.56

Unit 5 Power numbers

1 a) 2^1 b) 2^4
   c) 2^3 d) 2^0
   e) 2^6 f) 2^5
   g) 2^7

2 a) 3^1 b) 3^5
   c) 3^3 d) 3^2
   e) 3^0 f) 3^4
   g) 3^6

3 a) 4^3 b) 10^3
   c) 2^8 d) 7^3
   e) 6^3 f) 13^0
   g) 5^3 h) 11^3

4 a) 2^8 b) 3^4
   c) 2^9 d) 5^4
   e) 10^8 f) 4^{13}
   g) 7^{36} h) 3^2
   i) 5^{-5} j) 11^{-11}
   k) $3^5 \times 4^{11}$ l) $9^{16} \times 7^{-3}$
   m) $13^6 \times 8^{-4}$ n) $5^{14} \times 3^2 \times 6^5$
   o) $(3.1)^{11} \times (3.2)^6$

5 a) 4^1 b) 5^4
   c) 4^3 d) 7^4
   e) 2^{12} f) 6^{-1}
   g) 9^2 h) 5^{13}
   i) 7^1 j) 13^3
   k) $5^1 \div 6^{-3}$ l) $11^6 \div 9^{-5}$
   m) $3^{-20} \div 10^8$ n) $7^4 \div 5^{-10} \div 8^8$
   o) $(1.7)^{-5} \div (1.6)^{12}$

6 a) 8^{-3}
   b) 2^7
   c) 7^{-1}
   d) 9^{-19}
   e) 3^{-14}
   f) $7^{-2} \times 8^{-6}$
   g) $13^{-2} \div 2^{-7}$
   h) $5^{-4} \times 2^{12}$
   i) $9^6 \div 7^2 \times 10^{-4}$
   j) $(2.1)^1 \times (2.7)^{16}$

7 a) 2^7 b) 3^5
   c) 4^9 d) 5^8
   e) 6^6 f) 7^7
   g) 8^4 h) 9^5
   i) 11 j) 12

8 a) 9 b) $3^2 \times 8^4$
   c) 4×7^7 d) $5^4 \times 6^4$
   e) $3^3 \times 2^6$ f) 5×4^3
   g) 8×7 h) $10^5 \times 9$
   i) $2^5 \times 4$ j) $3^3 \times 5^6$

9 a) 4×10^2 b) 5×10^3
   c) 5.3×10 d) 7.8×10^2
   e) 9.4×10^4 f) 1.43×10^5
   g) $8.228\,22 \times 10^5$ h) 7.63×10
   i) 1.459×10 j) 6.37×10
   k) 4.895×10^2 l) $3.454\,454 \times 10^6$
   m) 3.5008×10 n) 7.823×10^3
   o) $7.439\,2 \times 10^4$ p) $6.923\,746 \times 10^6$
   q) 4.7×10^7 r) 5.239×10^2
   s) 8.274×10^3

10 a) 4×10^{-2} b) 7×10^{-4}
   c) 5.83×10^{-3} d) 9.02×10^{-2}
   e) 6.9×10^{-5} f) 4.5×10^{-8}
   g) 4.8×10^{-3} h) 1.72×10^{-2}
   i) 3.7×10^{-6} j) 6.009×10^{-3}

11 a) 3.3×10^2 b) 5.27×10
   c) 7×10^0 d) 2.4×10^{-1}
   e) 9.99×10^7 f) 6.183×10^3
   g) 6.53×10^{-1} h) 6.785×10^5
   i) 3.67×10^5 j) 3.25×10^{-5}
   k) 8.67×10^{-3} l) 1.24×10^{-2}
   m) 4.823×10^{-8}

12 a) 2.07×10^8 b) 2.288×10^{-6}
   c) 1.768×10^0 d) 8.35×10^{-9}
   e) 2.571×10^7 f) 1.6×10^8
   g) 3.052×10^{12} h) 1.98×10^{13}
   i) 1.435×10^{-1} j) 4.872×10^7
   k) 2.844×10^{18} l) 3.234×10^{-11}
   m) 1.8×10^5 n) 2.15×10^{14}
   o) 6.5×10^6 p) 4.2×10^{12}
   q) 6.5×10^{11} r) 2.5×10^{-10}

13 6.7483×10^7 people

14 1.53832×10^8 people

Unit 6 Other number systems

1
a) 57
b) 81
c) 23
d) 7
e) 94
f) 45
g) 36
h) 18
i) 39
j) 88
k) 66
l) 44
m) 29
n) 51
o) 14
p) 72
q) 95
r) 33
s) 12
t) 9

2
a) 449
b) 373
c) 114
d) 206
e) 482
f) 369
g) 172
h) 205
i) 326
j) 111
k) 1458
l) 3905
m) 2033
n) 3096
o) 2557
p) 1965
q) 3881
r) 1774
s) 2898
t) 3522

3
a) LXXIX
b) XIII
c) XLVI
d) XI
e) XXVI
f) LXVII
g) LVIII
h) XXX
i) LIV
j) XXII
k) LXXVII
l) XXXVIII
m) XLI
n) LXXV
o) XXXIV
p) XCVI
q) XVII
r) LV
s) XXXIV
t) XIX

4
a) DCLXI
b) DXCV
c) CCCXXXVI
d) CDXXVIII
e) DCIV
f) DLXXXI
g) CCCXCIV
h) CCXXVII
i) DXLVIII
j) CCCLXXII
k) MMDLXIX
l) MXVI
m) MMMCXLIV
n) MCVII
o) MMMDCLXVIII
p) MMCLXXVI
q) MCMXCII
r) MMDCCCLXXXV
s) MMMCMIX
t) MDCXXXIII

Unit 7 Approximation and estimation

1
a) i) 41 860   ii) 41 900   iii) 42 000
b) i) 553 360   ii) 553 400   iii) 553 000
c) i) 671 100   ii) 671 100   iii) 671 000
d) i) 1 156 120   ii) 1 156 100   iii) 1 156 000
e) i) 3 580 070   ii) 3 580 100   iii) 3 580 000
f) i) 771 140   ii) 771 100   iii) 771 000
g) i) 938 730   ii) 938 700   iii) 939 000
h) i) 39 050   ii) 39 000   iii) 39 000
i) i) 899 990   ii) 900 000   iii) 900 000
j) i) 3 786 670   ii) 3 786 700   iii) 3 787 000
k) i) 66 840   ii) 66 800   iii) 67 000
l) i) 491 130   ii) 491 100   iii) 491 000
m) i) 2 279 980   ii) 2 280 000   iii) 2 280 000
n) i) 87 747 810   ii) 87 747 800   iii) 87 748 000
o) i) 510   ii) 500   iii) 1000

2
a) 570 g
b) 800 g
c) 4 mm
d) 240 000 people
e) 29
f) 40 m
g) 23.5 cm
h) 5400 pupils
i) 960 km
j) 33.7 kg

3
a) 7.3
b) 31.0
c) 45.4
d) 38.0
e) 57.2
f) 249.1
g) 47.2
h) 3.5
i) 29.6
j) 227.8
k) 25.3
l) 3.1

4
a) 5.80
b) 37.90
c) 0.06
d) 25.05
e) 2.52
f) 3.45
g) 21.20
h) 9.10
i) 5.19
j) 23.60
k) 7.93
l) 239.35

5 a) 1.149   b) 9.556
    c) 21.617   d) 8.552
    e) 22.750   f) 7.939
    g) 33.758   h) 43.140
    i) 24.562   j) 5.937
    k) 1.697   l) 0.009

6 a) 6.8866   b) 1.20
    c) 0.337   d) 0.0008
    e) 0.05   f) 48.239
    g) 1.8   h) 0.0040
    i) 26.0   j) 834.69
    k) 1.422   l) 99.60

7 a) 3   b) 4
    c) 2   d) 4
    e) 1   f) 5
    g) 2   h) 2
    i) 5   j) 1
    k) 3   l) 5
    m) 3   n) 2
    o) 4   p) 4
    q) 1   r) 3
    s) 2   t) 2

8 a) 5.15   b) 3.68
    c) 7200   d) 0.800
    e) 0.006 00   f) 0.0880
    g) 29.1   h) 4.12
    i) 0.009 28   j) 0.0437

9 a) 251.2   b) 38.90
    c) 0.090 50   d) 701 000
    e) 1.946   f) 6005
    g) 29.25   h) 350.0
    i) 50 000   j) 3.007

10 a) 4.1   b) 2.595
    c) 0.004   d) 30
    e) 4.2   f) 0.68
    g) 0.0679   h) 328.01
    i) 4.70   j) 26.80
    k) 0.0047   l) 7.0
    m) 0.046   n) 29.0
    o) 9.5   p) 230.51
    q) 5.94   r) 23
    s) 0.060   t) 0.090
    u) 0.0202   v) 0.204
    w) 3 000 000   x) 5.0
    y) 0.07

11 a) i) 109.124   ii) 109
    b) i) 6.775   ii) 6.77
    c) i) 0.056   ii) 0.0563
    d) i) 44.582   ii) 44.6
    e) i) 1.780   ii) 1.78
    f) i) 359.240   ii) 359

12 a) i) 0.2280   ii) 0.2280
    b) i) 0.4360   ii) 0.4360
    c) i) 0.0577   ii) 0.057 65
    d) i) 36.2012   ii) 36.20
    e) i) 58.3932   ii) 58.39

13 8 pens

14 4 minibuses

15 15 pictures

16 13 bags

17 3 boxes

18 a) 1800   b) 1 800 000
    c) 400 000   d) 3 500 000
    e) 140 000   f) 5.6
    g) 280 000 000   h) 500
    i) 175   j) 0.175
    k) 1 000 000   l) 3

19 a) 80   b) 10
    c) 100   d) 2
    e) 200 000   f) 0.006
    g) 50   h) 80
    i) 6   j) 0.002
    k) 1000   l) 20

20 1600 pupils

21 600 km

22 a) $3000   b) $34 800

23 $1100

Unit 8 Measures and measurement

1 a) 288 hours
   b) 300 minutes
   c) 690 minutes
   d) $6\frac{1}{2}$ minutes
   e) $4\frac{1}{4}$ days
   f) $9\frac{3}{4}$ hours
   g) $4\frac{1}{3}$ hours
   h) 1020 seconds
   i) $3\frac{1}{3}$ days
   j) $7\frac{1}{4}$ hours
   k) 6240 minutes
   l) 24 600 seconds

2 a) 9 hours 28 minutes
   b) 9 hours 55 minutes
   c) 12 hours 21 minutes
   d) 33 hours 4 minutes
   e) 16 hours 19 minutes
   f) 19 hours 15 minutes

3 a) 5 hours 25 minutes
   b) 3 hours 9 minutes
   c) 1 hour 49 minutes
   d) 2 hours 55 minutes
   e) 7 hours 28 minutes
   f) 5 hours 56 minutes

4 a) 10 13   b) 09 46
   c) 00 27   d) 01 38
   e) 06 19   f) 14 37
   g) 16 55   h) 19 16
   i) 22 21   j) 20 40

5 a) 1.10 a.m.   b) 5.50 a.m.
   c) 12.10 a.m.   d) 10.40 a.m.
   e) 12.20 p.m.   f) 6.06 p.m.
   g) 3.15 p.m.   h) 7.09 p.m.
   i) 9.21 p.m.   j) 11.59 p.m.

6 a) 6 hours
   b) 12 hours 30 minutes
   c) 2 hours 45 minutes
   d) 7 hours 40 minutes
   e) 7 hours 52 minutes
   f) 10 hours
   g) 12 hours 15 minutes
   h) 11 hours 25 minutes
   i) 1 hour 45 minutes

7 a) 14 hours
   b) 19 hours 15 minutes
   c) 21 hours 30 minutes
   d) 11 hours 40 minutes
   e) 35 hours 23 minutes
   f) 9 hours
   g) 18 hours 45 minutes
   h) 16 hours 29 minutes
   i) 1 hour 18 minutes

8 6 hours 43 minutes

9 a) $3.60   b) $41.85

10 a) 6.45 p.m.   b) $6.80

11 a) 7.38 a.m.   b) 6.12 p.m.
   c) 8 hours 38 minutes

12 6 hours 10 minutes

13 a) 7.30 a.m.   b) 4.30 p.m.
   c) 54 hours

14 a) 500 cm   b) 6000 m
   c) 4000 mm   d) 81 230 mm
   e) 7.2 cm   f) 6.724 m
   g) 320 mm   h) 6100 m
   i) 7350 mm   j) 0.804 km
   k) 0.006 14 km   l) 0.147 m
   m) 7160 cm   n) 85.9 mm
   o) 5840 cm   p) 67 000 mm
   q) 9 300 000 cm   r) 37 800 mm
   s) 35 700 m   t) 527.5 mm
   u) 17 800 mm   v) 2 387 500 cm

15 7.748 m

16 16.388 km

17 a) 7900 g   b) 3.762 t
   c) 6375 g   d) 853 000 kg
   e) 0.329 t   f) 4460 kg
   g) 9875 kg   h) 0.074 kg
   i) 3.026 g   j) 5638 mg
   k) 0.000 863 t   l) 560 g

18 630 g

19 3.14 g

20 23.4 mg

21 2.8754 t

22 a) 93.534 litre   b) 84 000 ml
   c) 3796 ml   d) 26 915 ml
   e) 3.978 litre   f) 9.557 litre
   g) 17 625 ml   h) 154 750 ml
   i) 0.0473 litre

23 2175 ml

24 0.515 litre

Unit 9 An introduction to algebra

1 a) **E** $5x - 8$ b) **F** $5(x + 8)$
   c) **C** $8x + 5$ d) **A** $8(x + 5)$
   e) **D** $2(5x + 8)$ f) **G** $\frac{5}{8}x + 2$
   g) **B** $8(2x - 5)$

2 a) $9c + 5d$
   b) $6j^2 - 2g^2$
   c) $5a^2 + 4b^2$
   d) $7x + \frac{1}{3}yz$
   e) $2s - 17$
   f) $6c - 11$
   g) $\dfrac{4d}{8 + e}$
   h) $8(f + 4g) - \dfrac{b}{2k}$
   i) $2(e + 30) - 40$
   j) $\dfrac{2}{3}\left(n + \dfrac{3p}{7}\right)$
   k) $ab - 2(c - d)$
   l) $(y + 6) + 5$
   m) $\dfrac{2s + 5}{s}$
   n) $5 + \dfrac{t + 3}{2}$
   o) $\dfrac{15}{m + 12}$

3 a) 60   b) 20
   c) 7   d) 26
   e) 62   f) 22
   g) 100   h) 8
   i) 5   j) 0
   k) 24   l) 81
   m) 90   n) 32
   o) 1

4 a) $-\frac{1}{5}$ b) $-1\frac{1}{2}$
   c) $-3\frac{1}{4}$ d) $-1\frac{5}{6}$
   e) $-\frac{5}{6}$ f) $-\frac{8}{11}$
   g) $-\frac{16}{21}$ h) $-\frac{7}{36}$

5 a) $5y + 4$
   b) $7 - 3x$
   c) $-6y - 4$
   d) $10x - 6$
   e) $8x - 3y$
   f) $6x + y - 3$
   g) $-x - 2y + 7$
   h) $9 + 6x + 7y$
   i) $x - y - 12$
   j) $5x + 6 - 10y$
   k) $-4x + 4y - 9$
   l) $-3x + 11 - 4y$
   m) $-7 + 4y - 3x$
   n) $7x - 6y + 9$

6 a) $3a^2 + a - 1$
   b) $2b^2$
   c) $x^3 + 4x^2 - x + 2$
   d) $-2xy + 3$
   e) $2a - ab - b$
   f) $-t - 5s$
   g) $5yz + z$
   h) $a^2 - b^2 + a - b$
   i) $19pqr - 3abc$
   j) a^2b
   k) $8abc$
   l) $3\frac{1}{2}ab + bc$
   m) $\frac{1}{4}x + 1\frac{1}{2}y + \frac{2}{3}z$

7 a) $3c + 3b + 2a$
   b) $2y$
   c) $7a^2 + 8c^2$
   d) $-2b^2 - 4k^2$
   e) $5cb + 2ab + 5ac$
   f) $3a^3 + 5b^3 + 2a^2 + 2b^2 + 4c$
   g) $9abc - 11bc + 7ac$
   h) $7ab^2 + 5a^2b - 3ab + 6bc$
   i) $17x^3 + 19x^2 + 3x - 5$
   j) $1\frac{1}{2}x^2yz - xyz^2$
   k) $\frac{1}{2}xy^2 + 1\frac{1}{4}xy$
   l) $\frac{2}{3}yz + \frac{1}{2}xyz - 1\frac{1}{2}xz$
   m) $3x^3 + 2x^2 - 8$
   n) $2x^3 - 16x^2 + 5x + 16$
   o) $-6x^3 - 2x^2 - 3x + 16$
   p) $11x^3 + 5x^2 + 3x - 5$
   q) $x^3 + x^2 - 10x + 11$

8 a) $-14mn$ b) $15ab$
c) $32b^2$ d) $-14k^2$
e) $\frac{2}{3}y^2$ f) $-3x^2$
g) $12uv$ h) $\dfrac{6b}{a}$
i) $\dfrac{4m}{3n}$ j) $-72a^2b$
k) $\dfrac{10x^3}{3y}$ l) $\dfrac{5c}{d}$
m) $30d^3e^2f$ n) $-\dfrac{4b^2}{3a}$
o) $1\frac{1}{3}g^2$

9 a) $4m - 36$
b) $14f - 42$
c) $15k - 30m$
d) $6x + 8$
e) $12p + 18q$
f) $15d - 10e$
g) $x + y$
h) $x - y$
i) $3 - b$
j) $-9r - 3s$
k) $6n - 4m$
l) $-18p - 54$
m) $3r - 6s$
n) $5x - 2y$
o) $10x - 24$
p) $-8m - 1$

10 a) $14a - 27$
b) $6b + 23$
c) $5c + 3$
d) $16 - 3e$
e) $22f + 24$
f) $4g - 12$
g) $-10b - 11$
h) $27k - 1$
i) $21 - m$
j) $15n + 18$
k) $3p - 10q$
l) $11s - 21r$
m) $31t + 27u$
n) $3w - 11v$
o) $18y - 100x$
p) $55z - 15y$

11 a) $x^2 + 4x + 6$
b) $a^2 - 2a + 6$
c) $b^2 - 4b - 5$
d) $4c^2 - 25$
e) $d^2 - 9d + 18$
f) $-e^2 - e - 12$
g) $10x^2 - 11x$
h) $-6x^2 + 21x$
i) $12x^2 - 10x$
j) $5x^2 + 15x$
k) $14n^2 + 36n$
l) $17n - 12n^2$
m) $8n^2 + 32n$
n) $k^2 - 11k$
o) $34k - 13k^2$
p) $-7k^2 + 36k + 1$
q) $2k^2 + 7k$
r) $y^2 + 52y$
s) $14y^2 + 21y$

12 a) $3y^2 + 21y$
b) $12y^2 - 2y$
c) $-26u^2 + 25u$
d) $-42u^2 + 42u$
e) $13u^2 - 7u$
f) $17x^2 - 38x$
g) $7x^2 - 29x$
h) $-4t^2 + 68t$
i) $-40t^2 + 23t$
j) $-16p^2 - 30p$
k) $17t^2 + 12t$
l) $-23t^2 - 32t$
m) $13b^2 + 15b$
n) $4b^2 + 27b$
o) $-13b^2 - 10b$
p) $-14n^3 + 11n^2$
q) $-20n^3 + 51n^2$
r) $12a^4 - 6a^3 - 6a^2$

Unit 10 An introduction to geometry

1 a) 81° **b)** 23°
   c) 38° **d)** 42°
   e) 74°
2 a) 91° **b)** 7°
   c) 79° **d)** 163°
   e) 146°
3 a) $c = 67°$ **b)** $c = 55°$
   c) $c = 76°$ **d)** $c = 31°$
   e) $c = 27°$ **f)** $c = 41°$
   g) $c = 26°$ **h)** $c = 7°$
   i) $c = 52°$ **j)** $c = 36°$
   k) $c = 8°$ **l)** $c = 24°$
   m) $c = 24°$ **n)** $c = 28°$
   o) $c = 12°$ **p)** $c = 26°$
4 a) $s = 69°$ **b)** $s = 42°$
   c) $s = 76°$ **d)** $s = 159°$
   e) $s = 79°$ **f)** $s = 62°$
   g) $s = 72°$ **h)** $s = 40°$
   i) $s = 80°$ **j)** $s = 19°$
   k) $s = 37°$ **l)** $s = 33°$
5 a) $a = 50°$ **b)** $a = 41°$
   c) $a = 54°$ **d)** $a = 51°$
   e) $a = 15°$ **f)** $a = 26°$
   g) $a = 15°$ **h)** $a = 18°$
   i) $a = 80°$ **j)** $a = 15°$
   k) $a = 37°$ **l)** $a = 35°$
6 a) $g = 132°$
   b) $g = 65°$
   c) $g = 27°$
   d) $g = 36°$
   e) $g = 24°, h = 72°$
   f) $g = 18°$
   g) $g = 20°$
   h) $g = 20°, h = 100°$
   i) $g = 22°$
   j) $g = 23°$
   k) $g = 28°, h = 101°$
   l) $g = 9°, h = 23°$
7–14 Check pupils' constructions.

Unit 11 An introduction to coordinate geometry

1 Check pupils' graphs.
2 a) 1 **b)** 2
   c) -4 **d)** 3
   e) -2 **f)** 0
   g) $-2\frac{1}{2}$ **h)** $1\frac{1}{2}$
3 a) 4 **b)** -1
   c) -2 **d)** 0
   e) -3 **f)** $-3\frac{1}{2}$
   g) $\frac{1}{2}$ **h)** $1\frac{1}{2}$
4 $A(-4, 7)$ $B(3, 7)$
   $C(6, 5)$ $D(7, -3)$
   $E(0, -7)$ $F(-5, -5)$
   $G(-6, 2)$ $H(0, 4)$
   $I(6, 0)$ $J(2, -5)$
   $K(-2, -2)$ $L(-2, 0)$
5 a), b) Check pupils' graphs.
   butterfly
6 a) $A(-1, 1)$ $B(1, 2)$
   $C(3, 0)$ $D(-2, -2\frac{1}{2})$
   b) $A(-6, 2)$ $B(2, 6)$
   $C(4, 4)$
   c) $A(-1, 4)$ $B(1, 6)$
   $C(9, -2)$ $D(7, -4)$
   d) $A(-2, 4)$ $B(3, 5)$
   $C(4, -2)$ $D(-2, -4)$
   $E(-4, 0)$
   e) $A(0, 3)$ $B(4, 0)$
   $C(3, -3)$ $D(0, -5)$
   $E(-4, -2)$ $F(-3, 2)$
   f) $A\left(5\frac{1}{2}, 7\frac{1}{2}\right)$ $B\left(6\frac{1}{2}, \frac{1}{2}\right)$
   $C\left(5\frac{1}{2}, -1\frac{1}{2}\right)$ $D\left(\frac{1}{2}, -6\frac{1}{2}\right)$
   $E(-5, -4)$ $F\left(-7\frac{1}{2}, -\frac{1}{2}\right)$
   $G\left(-5\frac{1}{2}, 3\frac{1}{2}\right)$ $H\left(0, 6\frac{1}{2}\right)$
7 Check pupils' graphs.
   $D(3, 4)$
8 Check pupils' graphs.
   $D(-4, -3)$
9 Check pupils' graphs.
   $D\left(4, -1\frac{1}{2}\right)$
10 Check pupils' graphs.
   $D(-4, 2)$